THE TALENTED TENTH

BY RICHARD WESLEY

DRAMATISTS
PLAY SERVICE
INC.

THE TALENTED TENTH
Copyright © 1988, Richard Errol Wesley

NOTE ON BILLING

SPECIAL NOTE ON SONGS/RECORDINGS

THE TALENTED TENTH opened at the Manhattan Theatre Club (Lynne Meadow, Artistic Director; Barry Grove, Executive Producer) on November 9, 1989. It was directed by M. Neema Barnette; the scenic design was by Charles McClennahan; the costume design was by Alvin B. Perry; the lighting design was by Anne Militello; the sound design was by James Mtume; and the production stage manager was Diane Ward. The cast was as follows:

BERNARD	Roscoe Orman, Richard Lawson
PAM	Marie Thomas
ROWENA	LaTanya Richardson
TANYA	Akosua Busia, Lorraine Toussaint
MARVIN	Richard Gant
RON	Rony Clanton
GRIGGS	J. E. Gaines, Graham Brown

Notes on *The Talented Tenth*

The Black Power movement effectively ended sometime around 1974, and in its wake a new strain of black leadership elites emerged. They came from the business sector and the more traditional urban-ward politics sector. They eschewed the confrontational antiestablishment posture of Black Power, played down any overt identification with the African diaspora, and positioned themselves, basically, as centrist pragmatists. They might present an Afrocentric façade when it suited them—wearing a dashiki here, quoting Malcolm or Martin there—but for the most part, they saw themselves part of the system, as much a part of the "American way of life" as any other citizens.

The Black Power movement, in many ways, had cleared their path. Nearly a decade and a half of successful efforts at raising consciousness among black people and working to consolidate what little economic and political resources there were within the community made it possible for this new class to emerge, particularly when the Black Power movement withered as the result of COINTELPRO; national weariness with the excesses of the radical left; and the arrests, incarceration, and/or forced or self-imposed exile of many of the radical left's leaders.

The Public Accommodations Act was passed in 1964, the Voting Rights Act in 1965. Malcolm X and Martin Luther King were both dead and safely elevated to a sainthood that rendered their memories powerless and therefore nonthreatening. Suddenly, the question became, "Where do we go from here?" And while that question was being pondered by millions of black Americans, a new generation of black leadership quickly stepped forward to seize the reins of power in black America. Some were well-educated graduates of schools like Harvard or Wharton. Others were veterans of the Black Power movement, and still others emerged from the back rooms of ward politics in the big cities or the boardrooms of large corporations. They may have come from different backgrounds, but they all had many things in common, particularly erudition, intelligence, and ambition. They had labored long and hard in the background and had been patient. And now, in the aftermath of the hard-won social changes of the 1960s and 1970s, they were enjoying previously undreamed-of levels of success. I was a part of many of those circles, and had been since my very first day as a freshman at Howard.

By 1980, I was a man in his mid-thirties; married, with children; a homeowner; and in the middle of a successful professional career. I had not stood on a street corner with a crew since I was seventeen years old, and even then I had only been marginal. I would never know thug life the way Jay-Z or Biggie or Eazy-E would later come to exemplify. But I noticed that there was not much discussion on our stages about the "other half" of American black life—the middle class, the professional classes—and this observation was what led me to write a play that would address some of my observations about the emergence of this new class of leadership.

I originally intended for Essex Braxton, a major character in *The Mighty Gents*, to be a protagonist in the new play. The new play would occur on the very night that Braxton is assaulted by Frankie, Lucky, Tiny, and Eldridge. I imagined that, seeking to move up from being a mere criminal to being recognized as a successful business-man and investor, Braxton was on his way home from a party hosted by a well-heeled black professional. But I soon abandoned the idea altogether. I wanted to move in another direction.

The task would take me nearly ten years. I had to grow as a person as well as a writer. There were nuances of business practices, political dealmaking, and even interpersonal relationships that I needed to understand, both on the micro and the macro level.

The Talented Tenth became my take on what had happened to the former young soldiers of the Black Power movement of the '60s and early '70s, who now found themselves in their forties and successfully integrated into the American Dream. They had spacious homes, the requisite expensive cars, overseas vacations, excellent pension packages, and political connections—and still, something was missing. The bridge between the past and the present—between generations, social classes, interpretations of history, mother and daughter, father and son—has always been important to me. It is a theme that reverberates through every play I have ever written, but *Tenth* may have been the first time since my one-act play *The Past Is the Past* that I was so overt with it.

By the end of the 1970s, it was clear to everyone that an initial phase of the Black Power movement had run its course. There was not going to be a "revolution" in the streets. "The System" was not going to be overthrown and replaced by a more humane democratic socialism. That "fire in the belly" that had driven us in our youthful twenties and early thirties had now given way to a more practical sense of reality. The playwright Ed Bullins once said, "The most revolutionary thing any black man in America could do was to take care of his family." The truth of Ed's comment was borne out not only in statistics chronicling the deteriorating living conditions so many black Americans were facing at the time, but also in the police assassinations and arrests of scores of "militant black leaders and followers," as well as the personal failings of some of those leaders (cronyism, misogyny, and greed). And there was another factor equally important: fatigue—intellectual as well as physical and spiritual—giving way to cynicism and even despair. A new kind of strength was needed, a new vision. We came to realize that we were not going to save the world—at least, not yet.

One day, sometime in 1980–'81, I was invited by a good friend to attend the photography exhibition opening of another good friend (and former Howard classmate) who had developed a fine career for himself as a photographer. It was to be held in a suburban town just outside Newark, New Jersey. While I was there, chatting and talking with guests and friends, I suddenly became very aware of just who these people were: professionals in education, government, business, medicine, law, and law enforcement. Some of them came from families that had been established in the black communities of Essex County, New Jersey, for generations. And here I was, a working-class kid from Newark, rubbing shoulders with them. I'd only seen most from afar, or perhaps I'd read about them or heard them discussed while growing up. I may even have partied with some of their children in earlier years, but I never expected to really know much about them. But there I was. And just as comfortable and at ease as if I'd been with them all my life.

Ten years before, I'd have dismissed them as the "Black Bourgeoisie" and "Enemies of the Revolution." But the revolution had ended—or had it? Many of the young people in the room had marched, attended rallies; a few had even joined the Black Panthers.

Others had actually lived in Africa, something I'd never done. Some of the young women there had straightened their hair; others still wore it *au naturel.* Some of the men wore dashikis, while others preferred Brooks Brothers.

Howard University, the Movement, and a professional writing career that had allowed me to travel all over the country and to points overseas had all combined to mature me, and expose me to possibilities many other young black men my age were never destined to see. As I stood in that gallery on that long-ago day, I realized that I needed to write about these "new Negroes," because I was one of them.

The deaths of Malcolm X and Martin Luther King, combined with the end of "Black Power," created a leadership vacuum in the black American body politic. Into this stepped a new wave of young (and not so young), educated, sophisticated, and ambitious men and women, who saw themselves as less ideological than their forebears and more practical and pragmatic. They didn't want to destroy the system or overturn it. They wanted to assimilate into it.

Black Americans were as American as anyone else. All of the *Sturm und Drang* of the '60s was about just that. Our ancestors were in America centuries before the forebears of more than seventy percent of all the white people who called themselves Americans. Only the Native Americans had a greater claim to the American ideal than we did. We didn't need to go back to Africa. As James Brown famously said, "America is our home."

I decided to write a play about black, middle-class professionals, all of them former activists, who had settled into comfortable lives and were reaping the benefits of successful professional careers. But something is missing, and one of them, our protagonist Bernard, is determined to find that "something," so that he can reclaim the part of his life he feels he has lost.

W. E. B. Du Bois, in his seminal 1903 book *The Souls of Black Folk*, discussed the creation and elevation of a university-educated leadership class—roughly ten percent of the black population of the country, steeped in the liberal arts, enlightened philosophy, and science—who would lead the black masses to a stronger position in American society. They would establish the infrastructure for a newfound freedom. Realizing almost immediately how elitist this idea appeared, Du Bois abandoned it and never sought to promote it. But the "talented tenth" became part of the language of black communities for the next century. When I arrived at Howard in 1963, just one year after Du Bois' death, I remember some of my classmates and myself joking, upon realizing that so many of us were the first members of our families to go to college and that great expectations were held for all of us, that we were "The Talented Tenth."

I spent the entire decade of the '80s writing and rewriting this play. It was finished and placed into production—first at the Manhattan Theatre Club in 1989, and later, in 1990, at the Alliance Theatre in Atlanta as part of the National Black Arts Festival. Productions have followed all over the country since then. It would be the last full-length play I'd write for more than twenty years.

—R. W.

CHARACTERS

BERNARD
African American; late thirties, early forties.

PAM
Light-skinned African American; late thirties, early forties.

ROWENA
African American; late thirties, early forties.

TANYA
African American; mid-twenties.

MARVIN
African American; late thirties, early forties.

RON
African American; late thirties, early forties.

GRIGGS
African American; sixty-five to seventy years of age.

YOUNG MAN
African American; early twenties.

THE TALENTED TENTH

Scene 1

*The early 1990s. Lights up on a beach in Jamaica. Bernard,
Pam, Marvin, Rowena, and Ron relax in the sun.*

*Bernard stands apart from the others. Lights change and
we enter Bernard's memory. Griggs, here in his mid-fifties,
appears, dressed in a business suit.*

GRIGGS. Says here you went to Howard University.

BERNARD. *(Prideful smile.)* Just graduated.

GRIGGS. Fine school. Lotta good people have come out of there.
You know Professor Spaulding?

BERNARD. History Department?

GRIGGS. Yes.

BERNARD. I know of him. Never had him as a teacher.

GRIGGS. Good man, Spaulding. His father and I served in World
War II together.

BERNARD. I didn't know that.

GRIGGS. Course you didn't. It's not important. Tell me, Evans,
what are your goals in life?

BERNARD. My goals?

GRIGGS. Yes. I mean, what do you plan to do with your life?

BERNARD. *(Thinks a moment.)* Be a success.

GRIGGS. And?

BERNARD. Make lots of money.

GRIGGS. So I should hire you because you want to make lots of
money.

BERNARD. Well, uh—

GRIGGS. See, what you're talking about is a desire; it's not a goal. You have no concrete plan in place. Just some vague notion about lots of money, and you expect me to be the one to give it to you.

BERNARD. Well, no, Mr. Griggs. You see—

GRIGGS. Don't tell me, boy. I know what I see: Just one more pie-in-the-sky youngblood. "Be a success." "Make lots of money." I've heard that kind of talk before. It's Negroes daydreaming, that's all. Fantasizing. And fantasizing's dangerous for black people. Especially when they're young, like you. You want to work for me, you learn to look at this world with hard, cold eyes.

BERNARD. I think I understand, Mr. Griggs.

GRIGGS. Make sure you do, Mr. Evans, because school days are over. I run a successful business precisely because I have always understood how this world we live in is constructed. Especially for our people.

BERNARD. Things are changing, Mr. Griggs.

GRIGGS. And how would you know, youngblood? You just got here.

BERNARD. Well, sir, I know I can relax more in my life than my parents could in theirs.

GRIGGS. Relax? Hmph. Relax. So, that's what all our struggling has come down to: so you kids can relax.

BERNARD. Messed up again, didn't I?

GRIGGS. Hopeless. Just hopeless. The Race is in trouble. What is the primary arena in which our people's struggle must be won?

BERNARD. Civil Rights.

GRIGGS. Wrong. Generals who persist in using the tactics of the last war are doomed to defeat in the present one. Remember that. The correct answer is Economics, boy. Money begets power, and power can make anything possible in America.

BERNARD. Yes, Mr. Griggs.

GRIGGS. You don't believe me, but what I'm telling you is the truth. No individual in this country is more powerful than the ethnic group from which he comes. Don't you ever forget that. As long as the Negro is an economic cripple in America, I don't care how many laws are passed telling him what rights he has, I don't care how many of you colored whiz kids come dancing out of the Howards and Harvards of the world, it won't mean a thing if the majority of our people are outside the economic mainstream. Our job as Negro businessmen is to make money, be successful, and be a springboard for whatever is to follow. We have to be practical...and willing to hold on to our heads while everyone else around us is losing theirs. You understand what I'm saying to you?

BERNARD. I think so, Mr. Griggs.

GRIGGS. I'm talking about hard work, Mr. Evans. Really hard work. You young Negroes today have to understand that you have no rights, no privileges, no nothing.

BERNARD. Sir?

GRIGGS. All you've got is duty, responsibility, and the self-discipline that goes with it. It's the first seven generations after slavery that will suffer the most. They're the ones who have nothing to look forward to except struggle. They're the ones who have to bear the pain, make the sacrifices, and fight the battles that have to be fought and won. Your trouble will always come when you begin to think that you deserve a good time; when you begin to think that the world is your oyster. You're generation number six, Mr. Evans. Your grandchildren can have the good time. Not you. For you, there's only struggle. Understand?

Griggs begins moving away.

BERNARD. You frightened me when you said that.

GRIGGS. I know.

BERNARD. I've been frightened ever since.

Griggs is gone. Lights change. Pam, Rowena, Marvin, and Ron sun themselves on beach towels. Bernard remains standing to the side, staring out to sea. Easy-listening jazz plays on a portable cassette player.

PAM. You say something, honey?

BERNARD. Uh...no. Just thinking out loud.

ROWENA. I just love Negril.

MARVIN. I could stay here forever.

13

ROWENA. Shoot, you'd still have to work to make a living. Then, it wouldn't be fun here, anymore. Jamaica'd just be another place to work.

MARVIN. I'll take that chance.

PAM. I don't know. The poverty here depresses me. It's so pervasive. I couldn't stand it, every day.

BERNARD. Hmph. Seems like everywhere you go in the world, black people are suffering.

ROWENA. At least here, black folks are in control of their own lives.

BERNARD. No, they're not. The World Bank is.

RON. Actually, the Bahamas is what's happenin'. I'm planning a hook-up with some foreigners I know—an Arab and two Italians. I'm looking at some beachfront property on one of the outer islands— a resort.

ROWENA. But, Ron, you need contacts in the Bahamas, and you don't know anybody in Nassau.

RON. Rowena, there are black folks in Nassau with money and power. Wherever there are black people with money and power, there you will find a Howard graduate. All I need to do is knock on a few doors at Government House and do a little alumni networking.

MARVIN. Smart move.

RON. Only move there is, my man. Only move there is.

PAM. You make it sound so easy.

RON. No, it's not easy. It's hard work. But things have a way of coming together when you know what it is you want and how to go about getting it.

PAM. Business and money. Ugh! Please, we're on vacation. It's so vulgar to talk about that stuff when you're on vacation.

RON. It's in my blood. I can't help it.

ROWENA. We need to get you married off, Ron.

MARVIN. Oh, oh, marriage: the ultimate business entanglement.

ROWENA. Hardy-har-har. Very funny.

RON. I've been that route. No, thanks.

ROWENA. You need an anchor in your life.

14

RON. In my life, not around my neck.

PAM. What a sexist thing to say.

RON. All I'm saying is, I tried marriage. It was a disaster, for me *and* Irene.

PAM. That was ten years ago.

ROWENA. Then it's time you jumped in the waters again. All these intelligent eligible women out here and you walking around single. It's criminal.

RON. I'm doing fine, y'all.

PAM. Bernard, what do you think?

BERNARD. About what?

RON. They're trying to marry me off again.

BERNARD. *(Disinterested.)* Well, you'll do what you want to do, Ron. You always have.

ROWENA. Don't you want to see little carbon copies of yourself running around?

RON. One of me in the world is enough.

BERNARD. You won't get any argument from me on that score, brother.

> *Ron looks at him. Others laugh.*

Sorry, Ron, but you walked right into that one. I couldn't resist.

RON. I owe you one, Bernard.

BERNARD. I'm sure you'll be paying me back first chance you get.

RON. Count on it.

BERNARD. Hey, let's leave Ron's social life alone. Surely, there must be some more interesting things we can talk about, or do.

ROWENA. Why? We're on vacation. We're not *supposed* to do anything or talk about anything interesting or "relevant." Too taxing.

RON. Yea, Bernard, chill out. Empty your brain, bro. Plenty of time to fill it up once we get back home.

BERNARD. Yea, that's right. Just lie around in this sand all the damned time doing nothing and talking inanities. We do this year after year.

RON. It's never bothered you before.

BERNARD. It bothers me, now.

Beat.

Listen…I'm sorry.

PAM. Bernard, what is it?

BERNARD. Nothing.

MARVIN. Worried about old man Griggs and your promotion?

BERNARD. *(Evasively.)* It's hot.

MARVIN. Don't worry about that promotion. You'll get it. You're due.

BERNARD. It's not the promotion. *(Looking away.)* It's the aftermath.

RON. Aftermath? What's that about?

Bernard says nothing.

PAM. Why don't you let me get you something cool to drink?

BERNARD. Don't want a cool drink. I want to get off this damned spot I'm standing on. I want to get off this hot sand. I want to *move*. I want to *do* something.

PAM. Okay, let's do something. Any suggestions?

ROWENA. How about a game of whist?

BERNARD. *(A little incredulous.)* Whist?

ROWENA. *(Playfully.)* Yes, Bernard. You know, that ancient Negro parlor game.

BERNARD. No, let's drive over to Dunn's River Falls. There's a great restaurant there.

Groans from the others.

It's only a ninety-minute drive.

ROWENA. More like two hours, Bernard.

RON. Two hours in all this heat? I'm out, man.

ROWENA. Bernard, we've got a villa with our own cook and waiter. Why do we need to ride all that distance for a meal?

MARVIN. Ro's right. Chill, man. We've only got two days left here. Going to Dunn's River's gonna *waste* one of those days.

BERNARD. Negril is tourist Jamaica. It's not real. We need to get out and talk to the people, get to know them.

ROWENA. Get out and talk to the people? About what?

BERNARD. Maybe we can learn something about this lovely little island.

ROWENA. If it's so lovely, why are so many Jamaicans in Brooklyn?

BERNARD. For the same reason so many Alabamans are in Chicago.

Beat.

We could stop and see things. That's all I meant.

ROWENA. Right. The lovely drive along the North Coast Highway; endless miles of sugar plantations, shacks, outhouses, skinny dogs, goats, and ashy-faced children. Not me, honey. I'm staying right here in Negril. This may be tourist Jamaica to you, Bernard, but after paying my share for that villa and airfare and all the rest, this is all of Jamaica I have any interest in seeing. I'm sorry.

MARVIN. I wouldn't put it quite that bluntly, but my wife's got a point.

PAM. Bernard, stop standing over there all by yourself. Come lay beside me.

Bernard comes over to Pam and sits beside her. She pulls him down so that his head rests on her belly.

BERNARD. *(Sighs.)* Y'all just don't understand.

ROWENA. I understand this sun caressing my body, I'll tell you that. Let me turn over. I intend to be right black when I go back home.

Lights begin to change. Everyone lapses into a nap as the sounds of the surf crashing onto the beach with the seagulls flying overhead can be heard. Bernard sits up and stares out to sea.

Lights continue to change and segue to the next scene.

Scene 2

Lights up on Bernard, alone, putting a sweatsuit on over his beachwear.

BERNARD. It was during my junior year in college. Martin Luther King tried to lead a march across the Edmund Pettus Bridge in Selma, Alabama, but the local authorities had a law against it. Those were the days down south when there were laws against black people doing anything, including being black, if you get my drift. Well, Dr. King decided to march anyway, and the sheriff's people attacked the marchers and threw them in jail. People all over the country called on President Johnson to do something, but Johnson hesitated. Then, Dr. King announced he would march again, this time all the way to Montgomery, the state capital. The Klan started making noises. And Lyndon Johnson still hesitated. So, the Student Nonviolent Coordinating Committee went into action. They had a local chapter down on Rhode Island Avenue, not that far from the campus and Habiba and I went down there right after philosophy class and signed up together. We were ready, y'all.

I remember my heart was beating a mile a minute. The both of us were so excited. We were finally in the big fight: helping the Race in the Civil Rights Struggle. We were active participants in making History.

The room was filled with nervous energy. People sang civil rights songs and hugged each other and held hands—men and women, black and white.

Then came speeches and pronouncements to get us fired up. Lots of fists clenched in the air. The room was hot and sweaty and filled with cigarette smoke. I felt a little dizzy and reached for Habiba. Someone began singing "Precious Lord Take My Hand" and folks joined in. We all held hands and closed our eyes and let the power of the song take hold of us. Then, Habiba started shaking, gasping for breath, like she was convulsing. Suddenly, she opened her eyes and looked at me, saying she'd had a race memory. She was with a group of runaway slaves. Armed gunmen had chased them through a swamp. They were trapped with no way out. They began

18

to sing, calling out to God, and the more they sang, the stronger they became. She saw the flash of the gunfire. She felt the bullets searing into her flesh. But she kept getting stronger. Then, Habiba screamed. Just like that. A scream like I'd never heard before. Everyone in the room just stopped. It was like we all felt what she felt. People began to moan and shout and chant. Bloods who'd stopped going to church and had sworn off the spirit possession of our parents and grandparents began to rock and shake and tremble— yea, they got the Spirit that night! All that college sophistication we had didn't mean a thing! 'Cause Dr. King needed us! The workers down in Mississippi needed us! Our people needed us! Yes sir! We were gonna press on, that night! Ol' Lyndon Johnson, you better listen to us, man! 'Cause we comin'! Marching around your front lawn tonight, buddy! And you're gonna send those troops down to Selma and you're gonna sign that civil rights bill, too! Our time is at hand! This is the new young America talkin' and you'd better listen! Scream, Habiba! Scream, sister! Let us feel those bullets! Let us feel the lash! Scream! Don't let us forget! Bring us home, sister love! Bring us home! Yes sir! Yes sir! Teach! Teach!

Pause.

We marched in shifts, twenty-four hours a day, seven days. Lyndon Johnson sent the troops and Dr. King made his pilgrimage to Montgomery where he gave one of the greatest speeches of his life. Still see that speech from time to time on TV. I was listening to it the other day when my oldest son came in and asked me if I could give him some money for new clothes. School was out and they were having a special holiday sale at the mall. Martin Luther King's birthday.

Lights come up full to reveal Bernard in Tanya's living room as we segue to:

19

Scene 3

Bernard, alone, wearing a sweatsuit, seated in front of a TV set.

BERNARD. Come on, come on…get a hit.

ANNOUNCER. Strike! On the outside corner.

BERNARD. Strike?! That ball was outside. Damn!

> *Tanya enters, wearing a negligee. She is in her mid-twenties; dark-complexioned; brown, almond-shaped eyes; high cheekbones. She carries a can of beer and sits next to Bernard, who is still absorbed in the game. Tanya hands him the beer.*

Thanks, baby.

TANYA. Thought you were coming back inside.

BERNARD. Yea…I was…but, I flipped on the TV to get the score and…

TANYA. Yes, I know; the rest is history. *(Disinterested.)* Who's playing?

BERNARD. Mets and Dodgers.

TANYA. Who's winning?

BERNARD. Tie score, bottom of the ninth. One out. Mets win if my man here hits one out.

TANYA. He's gonna strike out.

BERNARD. Don't say somethin' like that. You'll jinx him.

TANYA. He's jinxing himself. He's holding his bat too high and too far back. It's gonna take him too long to get the head of the bat through the strike zone.

BERNARD. No way. He always comes through in the clutch.

ANNOUNCER. Swing and a miss, strike three!

TANYA. Told you.

BERNARD. I hate it when you show off like that.

TANYA. *(Big grin.)* Yea. I know.

> *She kisses him. He responds, but not with much enthusiasm, and immediately gets back into the game.*

Baby, you've got some gray hair.

BERNARD. That's not gray. It's lint.

TANYA. You are *too* vain. This is gray hair.

BERNARD. Stress. You're wearing me out, baby.

TANYA. Then, why don't you come back inside and drink from my fountain of youth?

> *Bernard smiles, but doesn't move, keeping his eyes on the TV.*

You know you haven't said anything about your trip to Jamaica.

> *Bernard grunts.*

Not that I really care.

BERNARD. The trip was alright.

TANYA. Nothing happened down there, did it?

BERNARD. No.

TANYA. *(Muttering.)* Too bad. *(Looks at him.)* You didn't get too tired running, did you?

BERNARD. Only three miles. I can do that in my sleep. *(Into the TV.)* Hey! Way to go! Do it! Do it!

TANYA. *(Looks at the TV, indifferent.)* A triple. Not bad. The Mets'll win.

BERNARD. You never know.

TANYA. Look at that gap between left field and left center. Game over if one falls in there.

BERNARD. Tanya…

ANNOUNCER. That's quite a big gap in left and left center. A hit over there, Mets win.

TANYA. God, I'm good. *(To Bernard.)* When are you going to take me somewhere?

BERNARD. When I get time.

TANYA. You never seem to have any time.

BERNARD. I do the best I can, Tanya.

TANYA. You always have time for Pam.

BERNARD. She's my wife.

TANYA. Hmph.

BERNARD. *(To the TV.)* Come on, lay off that junk stuff and make him throw strikes.

TANYA. You know, I haven't seen you for two weeks. The least you could do is talk to me.

BERNARD. We talked earlier. I want to watch the game. Okay?

TANYA. You can watch the game with your wife.

BERNARD. Pam doesn't like baseball.

TANYA. So, you come here to take up MY time.

BERNARD. Well, the hell with it, then!

TANYA. *(Soothingly.)* Come on, Bernard, I'm only teasin'.

BERNARD. Look, I'm tryin' to relax. Okay? It's been a long day. I like to watch the game.

TANYA. I understand all that. It's alright.

> *Beat.*

But, you can see my point, can't you?

BERNARD. *(Impatiently.)* Yes, Tanya.

TANYA. I had lunch with an old classmate of mine.

BERNARD. *(Into the game.)* Uh-huh…

TANYA. She's an investment banker, now. Wall Street.

BERNARD. …Good for her…

TANYA. I want to go in with her on a real estate deal she's trying to hook up down south. What do you think?

> *Bernard says nothing.*

Look, is that game over?

BERNARD. They're going into extra innings.

TANYA. Lord, deliver me.

BERNARD. Thought you liked baseball.

TANYA. I was hoping we could *talk*.

BERNARD. We've *been* talking, baby.

TANYA. I mean, without interruptions.

BERNARD. Tanya, this is a good game.

> *Tanya goes to the TV.*

TANYA. Uh-uh. No way. Forget it.

She shuts off the TV.

BERNARD. Hey! What're you doing?!

TANYA. Later for the game. Touch my bases.

BERNARD. Come on, baby.

TANYA. *(Continuing to block the TV.)* No.

BERNARD. But, the game—

She kisses him.

That's what I've always liked about you, baby. You know how to put things in their proper perspective.

They caress and embrace each other.

TANYA. Mmmm...I think these arms must be the most comfortable place in the world. I'm gonna have a law passed: You have to keep these arms around me twenty-four hours a day.

BERNARD. You don't need to get a law passed for that, baby.

TANYA. No. All I need is a ring.

BERNARD. Uh...er...what time is it?

TANYA. About 10:30.

BERNARD. Time for me to get up from here.

TANYA. Will I see you tomorrow?

BERNARD. I don't know.

TANYA. When, then?

BERNARD. I'll call.

TANYA. You're gonna jog the three miles all the way home?

BERNARD. Why not? Ran all the way here, didn't I?

TANYA. It's so late.

BERNARD. No sweat. I can handle it.

TANYA. I can drive you.

BERNARD. No.

TANYA. I'll let you off at the corner. Don't worry. Your wife won't see you...or me.

BERNARD. I said, no.

TANYA. You look sleepy. You ought to rest awhile. Come curl up with me.

BERNARD. You know as well as I do, if I curl up with you, I ain't gon' hardly rest.

TANYA. I won't bother you. Honest. Just stay awhile.

BERNARD. You know I can't. I've got a busy day tomorrow.

TANYA. I'll wake you early enough.

BERNARD. I gotta go to the bathroom. The beer's catching up to me.

TANYA. Why don't you and Pam get a divorce?

BERNARD. Because I love her.

TANYA. Then, why are you here with me?

BERNARD. Because I love *you*.

TANYA. That's immature.

BERNARD. I gotta go pee.

He exits. Tanya flicks on the TV.

TANYA. Bernard, the game's still on.

She smiles sardonically, the irony in her statement suddenly striking her.

Scene 4

Lights up on Tanya, alone.

TANYA. My father is a truck driver. My mother runs a little three-table greasy spoon on Springfield Avenue that I had to help clean up every day from the time I was in the third grade right up until I graduated from college.

I grew up during the sixties and have therefore benefited from the concessions gained in those years without having to endure the hassles. As a result, I have certain expectations and I tend to take things for granted…*a lot*. Because I know how to fight, I know how to make my expectations come true. You see, I learned early that, being black *and* female, I was at the bottom of everybody's pecking order and, consequently, if I didn't grab what I wanted myself, it wouldn't get got.

I'm sort of a black cultural cybernetic organism. Yea, check that out. Inside, a strong inner-city core surrounded by the soft flesh of my parents' middle-class aspirations, my training at Spelman College, and my graduate study at Columbia School of Journalism. Today, I work at the largest newspaper in New Jersey. I even have a byline. I'm a child of my generation; a strong believer in the power of the Individual Will. *I* am indestructible.

In college, a group of us like-minded young indestructible women clustered ourselves into a little clique we called The Women of Substance. We wanted to differentiate ourselves from the so-called popular women, many of them daughters of the black professional elite. Serious old Negro money. You've all seen them: the ones with the coquettish smiles and the batting eyelashes. The ones who were always used to having things. Anything. Anytime, anyplace, anywhere, anyhow. They didn't know how to fight. They didn't have to. They just snapped their fingers and…voilà. This was especially true when it came to men.

We women of substance were everything the so-called popular women were not. We were well-read, hard-working, studious, dedicated…and after what they used to call "the high-priced spread." We just couldn't understand. We were women who could *do* things.

Then it became clear: Women who can do things are most prized by men who can do nothing. And the *men* who can do things want women who can do *nothing*. Because such women are no competition and are eternally grateful to these men for giving them station in life. I've become convinced the male ego is Mother Nature's idea of sick humor.

Thus, here I am: attractive, successful, intelligent, and alone. Kept on an emotional string by a man married to one of those "high-priced spreads." All I have to do is tell him it's over. I should, really. But, now, *I've* gotten used to having whatever I've wanted. And I want *him*.

This situation has taught me something I never thought it necessary to learn, being a black woman of substance—Patience. It's more than a virtue…it's a weapon.

Lights.

Scene 5

Lights up on Ron, Marvin, and Bernard at a bar.

RON and MARVIN. *(Singing.)*
  For he's a jolly good fellow!
  For he's a jolly good fellow!
  For he's a jolly good felloooooooow!
  Who really knows how to throw down!
  Bernard stands and acknowledges the toast.

BERNARD. Thank you, thank you. I deserve every bit of it.
  They laugh.

RON. Congratulations, homeboy. Vice president and general manager. I love the sound of it.

BERNARD. I love the *feel* of it.

RON. And to think, you damned near drove yourself crazy worryin' about that promotion.

MARVIN. Wear it well, buddy-buddy. You're the big cheese, now.

BERNARD. Yea, control over all four of my company's stations. Got it all, ya'll: programming, news, public affairs—all mine. And it's all gonna change. Starting next month, Negro radio is dead at Griggs Broadcasting.

MARVIN. Don't get too radical, bro.

BERNARD. I've got to get radical. Not one of our stations is ranked in the top ten in any of their markets.

MARVIN. Really? Didn't know things were that bad.

BERNARD. Our stations are ratings disasters. We made money last year, but we don't turn things around, those profits won't mean a thing.

RON. R&B during the day, Quiet Storm in the evening. Never fails.

BERNARD. I'll have music, but not twenty-four hours a day. I want to do confrontational radio. Crime, corruption, police brutality, lack of quality services—things our people think they can't do anything about, we'll teach them they can. Politics, art, culture—not

26

only will we cover them, but we'll define them…on our terms. Cutting-edge radio, Ron. That's what it's all about.

RON. You're off into some form of advocacy, Bernard. A very bad habit I thought you'd gotten out of years ago.

BERNARD. All Griggs has to do is say "yes" and I'll have things turned around in six months.

RON. Whatever you do, use a little diplomacy. Sam Griggs is one of the pioneer black businessmen in the country.

BERNARD. I don't need to be lectured on office etiquette, Ron. I know what I want and I'm going after it.

MARVIN. You might be moving too fast, Bernard.

BERNARD. None of our competitors interprets the news of history or *anything* that goes on in this country through the eyes of the black community or from the *interests* of the black community. It's the world the way white folks see it, whether they mean for it to be that way, or not. *That's* how it comes out. And that's what I'm challenging and that's what I'm changing. The minute that happens Griggs Broadcasting becomes unique and controversial. Controversy attracts people…and dollars. And if we do our jobs right, not *all* the people we attract will be black, either. Gimme credit for having some brains. Okay?

MARVIN. I still don't know…

BERNARD. Damned right, you don't know. Look, it's my responsibility. Let me handle it. Okay?

MARVIN. No need to get upset, my man. I was just voicing my opinion.

BERNARD. The kind of opinion that makes daring, innovation, and risk-taking such dirty words among black businessmen.

RON. Because capital is limited for most of us. Those hungry bankers always seem to lose their appetite when they see black faces. Griggs knows that, even if you don't.

MARVIN. Look, you just got a big promotion. All you gotta do is make the money and relax. That's all: Just relax.

BERNARD. Relax? Marvin, I want to be the most restless black man who ever lived.

Bernard tosses some bills on the counter.

I'm gonna split. Me an' Pam's got plans.

RON. Give her my best.

BERNARD. I'll be sure to.

RON. That's a good woman you got, man. First class all the way.

BERNARD. Yea. She's good people. I'm a lucky man.

Bernard gulps down his drink.

RON. *(Laughs.)* Listen to him. I should have married her when I had the chance.

MARVIN. You did have the chance, but she wanted Bernard.

RON. *(To Bernard.)* Still can't see what she saw in you.

BERNARD. *(Looks at Ron.)* Good looks beyond belief—

RON. She's not that shallow.

BERNARD. You guys watch that scotch. You both gotta drive tonight.

Bernard exits. Ron and Marvin's eyes follow him. Ron gulps down another drink.

RON. You know he's gonna blow it, don't you? Guys like him always do.

Scene 6

Pam and Bernard are having breakfast. She looks through the mail.

BERNARD. I'm thinking about going out to the stadium to see the ball game. Want to come?

PAM. Baseball?

BERNARD. Yea.

PAM. Can I think about it?

BERNARD. Sure…

He continues eating. She looks through the mail. Bernard looks at her.

Anything interesting?

PAM. Just the usual bills…junk mail… *(Looks at Bernard.)* I ran into Sylvia Witherspoon, yesterday.

BERNARD. How's she doing?

PAM. She told me you and her husband had a fight at the station.

BERNARD. It was an argument. Not a fight.

PAM. She said you've been arguing a lot, lately.

BERNARD. There are things I want to do, but can't. He's one of the reasons I can't.

PAM. Is there anyone there you're not fighting with?

BERNARD. Lots of people.

PAM. Bernard?

BERNARD. I had a nice time at the fundraiser last night.

PAM. *(Beat.)* No, you didn't have a nice time. You danced and talked. But you never really said anything to anyone. You did it all night. And, just now, to me. You're effecting a conversation in order to avoid having a real one.

BERNARD. Aw, Pam, come on…

PAM. Silences, changing the subject; empty jokes. All means of keeping people away from you. Everyone likes who they think is you. The dedicated ex-boy wonder who always seems on top of everything. But, I was thinking that, after fifteen years of marriage, I still don't even know what your favorite color is.

BERNARD. You never asked.

PAM. You never told me.

BERNARD. Dark blue. What's yours?

PAM. Pink.

BERNARD. I thought it was yellow.

PAM. It's pink.

BERNARD. I could have sworn it was yellow.

PAM. Pink.

BERNARD. You never even wear pink. Your favorite dress is yellow.

PAM. You see, you're doing it again.

BERNARD. Well, I'll be damned. Pink.

PAM. Bernard, I'm not just talking about pink or yellow or dark blue. Ron noticed it, too.

BERNARD. My alleged distance, I suppose.

PAM. Yes. We were talking.

BERNARD. You were talking about me?

PAM. After all these years he was surprised about how little he knew about you.

BERNARD. You were talking to Ron about me.

PAM. Yes. He's your friend, Bernard.

BERNARD. *(Sarcastic.)* So he is.

PAM. What's that supposed to mean?

BERNARD. Ron can get to be a bit much, Pam.

PAM. He's a success at what he does. He's happy, Bernard. So few of our people get the kinds of opportunities he's getting. Be glad for him. He's happy for us.

BERNARD. So, how about it?

PAM. What?

BERNARD. You want to go to the ball game with me?

PAM. Bernard, we were talking about—

BERNARD. Come on, Pam. You'll love it. Just give it a chance.

PAM. I hate sports. I don't understand sports. Besides, we're talking about—

BERNARD. The same ol' same ol'. Forget that stuff. I'll behave, next time. I promise. Let's deal with something I want, this time.

PAM. *(Sighs.)* Can we go out to dinner, afterwards?

BERNARD. Sure.

PAM. Then, I guess it'll be alright.

BERNARD. Your enthusiasm is overwhelming.

PAM. In America, it's sports, not religion, that's the opiate of the masses…the male masses, anyway.

BERNARD. Stop grumbling. I've got box seats on the first-base line, baby. Gift from one of our ad clients.

PAM. First-base line. Is that good?

BERNARD. The best seats in the house.

PAM. Somehow the phrase "best seats in the house" would work much better for me if it was applied to the Met or the Alvin Ailey.

BERNARD. For most of the people where I come from, the stadium IS the Met.

PAM. Their loss, I'm afraid.

BERNARD. Alright, the hell with it! Forget the ball game. Let's go wherever you want to go! You satisfied?

PAM. Bernard, I didn't mean—

BERNARD. Save it! We'll do whatever you want to do. I'll go get changed into something appropriate. Will a sports coat do, or must it be black tie and goddamned tails! We'll do whatever you want to do! Go wherever you say! After all, you're the one with the taste! You're the one with the sophistication and breeding! You're the one, you're the one, you're the one!!

Bernard slams the newspaper down, gets up, and storms out, leaving Pam sitting alone, trembling, confused, angry, and hurt.

Scene 7

Tanya's apartment, as she massages Bernard's temples.

TANYA. You've got too much pressure on you, honey. You need to relax.

BERNARD. I don't want to relax. I just—

TANYA. What?

BERNARD. *(Changes subject.)* I'm gonna take a coupla days away, I think. Maybe the Coast. Check on our sister stations.

TANYA. Can I go with you?

BERNARD. No.

TANYA. Is *she* going?

BERNARD. No.

31

TANYA. Then, why can't I go?

BERNARD. I want to go alone.

TANYA. I see.

BERNARD. Don't start with me, Tanya.

TANYA. I'm not starting anything. You want to go alone. Fine.

BERNARD. Got something I've got to work out.

TANYA. What things?

BERNARD. Let me worry about that.

TANYA. Am I involved?

BERNARD. Tanya…

TANYA. I don't know why you get like this.

BERNARD. I'm sorry I didn't make that party with you.

TANYA. You could have at least called.

BERNARD. It's hard for me to talk on phones.

TANYA. It's hard for you to talk in person.

BERNARD. I didn't want to call and say I wasn't coming. I didn't want to disappoint you. By not calling, I wouldn't have to deal with it.

TANYA. Well, you did disappoint me and you *do* have to deal with it.

BERNARD. I'm sorry.

TANYA. Why didn't you want to come?

BERNARD. It's not that I didn't want to come. I just couldn't.

TANYA. Your wife?

BERNARD. I didn't want to run into someone who knew me…or worse, knew Pam.

TANYA. That's bound to happen, sooner or later, Bernard.

BERNARD. Why let it happen, at all?

TANYA. You know, I'm getting tired of being your best-kept secret.

BERNARD. You have to expect it when you become a married man's mistress, Tanya.

TANYA. Don't you ever say anything like that to me again. I am *not* your mistress.

She rises and moves away from him.

BERNARD. I'm sorry. I didn't mean to hurt your feelings.

TANYA. I don't know how much longer I can keep this up.

BERNARD. Look, I told you if you wanted to call it quits, it was fine with me. You're a beautiful, intelligent woman—too beautiful and intelligent to be stuck up under a married man.

TANYA. Don't talk to me like I'm some smitten teen queen, Bernard. I'm not stuck up under you. I *chose* to be with you and I *choose* to have you in my life.

BERNARD. You may come to regret that choice.

TANYA. Don't think the thought hasn't occurred to me.

BERNARD. I'm looking for answers, Tanya. I don't even know how I got here, anymore.

TANYA. Where?

BERNARD. Here. This point in my life, remembering that once I was twenty-two, fresh out of college, with an unlimited horizon in front of me. Then, just like that, I was twenty-five, then suddenly thirty, then thirty-five…now, forty-three. How did it happen so fast? Everything in between seems like a haze, sometimes. I remember being skinny with jet-black hair and baby-smooth skin. It used to take me a whole week just to grow a stubble. I was just twenty-two… Now, it's all these years later and I'm scared and I'm angry because I want to change my life and do some things I've never had a chance to do. But, if I do I could hurt my wife and my children and everyone who depends on me, so I stay where I am and I dream. But, I don't dare *act*. And yet, I *want* to act… I've *got* to act…before it's too late.

TANYA. *(Beat.)* You can talk and philosophize all you want to; you can even pretend that this anxiety you're feeling is some sort of midlife crisis, but I know what you're really saying: You want to leave Pam.

BERNARD. I've tried to leave her. I can't.

TANYA. I know. You're loyal to her. That's what attracted me to you.

BERNARD. It's more than loyalty. She's a part of me.

TANYA. You love her.

BERNARD. That's what I tell myself.

TANYA. Don't you know?

BERNARD. We've been together seventeen years.

TANYA. You're sick.

BERNARD. Sick?

TANYA. No. Not sick. Selfish.

BERNARD. Because I don't know my own feelings?

TANYA. You know your own feelings, alright. You like the idea that you can be married to one woman while having an affair with another, then expecting both of them to somehow be forgiving because you refuse to choose. Why should you choose? You're having the best of both worlds. Meanwhile, your wife and I suffer.

BERNARD. Then, why do you stay with me?

TANYA. Because I love you.

BERNARD. It's not enough. Take it from one who knows.

TANYA. I don't know anything deeper than love. I haven't lived that long. *(Looks into his eyes.)* You want it to end between us, don't you?

BERNARD. If you had seen the way I went off on Pam—

TANYA. I don't care about Pam. Don't tell me a damned thing about you and her. I only care about us. You want to end it?

BERNARD. We should. I can't carry this around with me any longer.

TANYA. It hasn't been easy for me, either, Bernard.

BERNARD. I'm sorry.

TANYA. Just like that, huh? I should have seen it coming.

> *Bernard says nothing.*

I was never happier with anyone than I was with you.

BERNARD. I'd better go…

TANYA. No! Look me in the face. Tell me you don't love me anymore. Tell me you don't want to be around me anymore.

> *Bernard comes face to face with her.*

BERNARD. I don't love you anymore.

TANYA. Just like that.

BERNARD. What other choice do I have? I won't leave my wife

and children, and I can't ask you to wait for me forever. Let's just stop it, now.

TANYA. I know you're right. I know there's no other way.

BERNARD. I'm sorry. It's my fault. I've been a fool.

TANYA. Maybe we've both been fools.

BERNARD. Yes.

TANYA. Goodbye.

BERNARD. Goodbye.

> *He turns to leave. Then, suddenly, he turns back and grabs Tanya into his arms. They kiss passionately, falling to the floor and making love. The lights dim.*

Scene 8

> *Lights up on Rowena and Pam relaxing in a sauna. Rowena seems content but Pam is distracted, distant.*

ROWENA. ...so, I wind up spending the whole morning on the phone with that Tommy Barrett in the city planner's office.

PAM. Betty Lee Barrett's son? The parks commissioner?

> *Rowena nods her head.*

You need to stay away from those Barretts. That's one ignorant family.

ROWENA. I called that boy to talk about the bid I put in for those vacant lots over in Woodlawn, and that little pootbutt tried to give me the runaround.

PAM. I'm not surprised.

ROWENA. Here, I've got the financing together to put up one thousand units of low- to moderate-income housing and all I get from city hall is a lot of bureaucratic nonsense about feasibility studies and background checks. Well, I know a background he can *kiss*!

PAM. They've made a deal somewhere, Ro. You've been elbowed out the way.

35

ROWENA. I know. Rumor has it some suburban big shot with big bucks greased the right palms. Bad enough when white politicians mess over you, but to get done in by one of your own... Damn.

PAM. Well, nothing in the rule books says black politicians have to be any less greedy than the white ones.

ROWENA. My rule book says they do. We put them there to do a job, and make our lives better; not screw us around like everyone else has done.

PAM. I'll remember to tell that to Mayor Mitchell next time I see him.

ROWENA. And while you're at it, ask him about that twenty-two-year-old youth counselor I hear he got pregnant. And ask him about Andy Thompson getting busted in that school jobs kickback scandal. And ask him about those coke sniffers he got on his very staff that he's not willing to do anything about. And then he's got the nerve to let some party hacks' snot-nosed kid block my housing project. I'm just two seconds away from getting the biggest base-ball bat I can find and going down to city hall to do some urban renewal on those stupid Negroes' *heads!*

Rowena and Pam have a laugh and exchange high fives.

PAM. Do yourself a favor: Next time, forget Tommy Barrett. Go straight to the top and talk to Georgie Mitchell. He's the mayor.

ROWENA. I intend to.

PAM. Watch him, though. He's slick.

ROWENA. Shoot, Georgie doesn't worry me. I always could handle a man who thinks with his little head instead of his big one.

Rowena laughs again. Pam is much quieter this time.

Ooowee! Don't get me started, girl.

The laughter dies down. Rowena looks at Pam.

Well, have we beat around the bush enough, or are you going to talk about what's bothering you?

PAM. Nothing's bothering me. I'm fine.

Rowena looks at her.

Am I that transparent?

ROWENA. What's going on, girl?

PAM. I was never raised to air dirty linen in public. It just wasn't done in my family.

> *Beat.*

Me and Bernard are going through a thing, that's all. It's nothing. *(Beat; quietly.)* It's been going on for months. He's been real moody...distant. Snaps at me...sometimes, even the kids. He'll sit at the dinner table and stare off into space—won't even take part in the family discussions...he used to lead them.

ROWENA. Have you talked to him about it?

PAM. I can't *get* him to talk. It's like he's stopped connecting with me. Left me on a little island. I can't figure him anymore. It's like he never says what's really on his mind.

ROWENA. Maybe he does, and you just don't understand him. I do that with Marvin, sometimes.

PAM. I *know* Bernard. We've been married seventeen years. This just isn't like him.

ROWENA. Now, how many women have made *that* mistake. Hmph, I know I have... "I know my husband." Like I know Marvin better than he knows himself. Really... We devote so much of our time to studying our men, trying to figure out what makes them tick, knowing what they're going to say, how they're going to react in certain situations. And just when we get everything down pat, when we think we have that man arranged just the way we want him, he'll say something, or do something or even worse, do nothing, at all. And then we realize, we never really knew him. We only loved him.

PAM. There are times when I can feel his eyes on me. Going over every inch of my body. What's he looking for? I can feel myself getting older. Sometimes, it seems as though I can feel my hair turning gray; I can feel the natural oils in my skin drying out. And I wonder if that's the reason he looks at me so strangely. Maybe that's why he's changed. And I come to this gym hoping I can turn the clock back and then I see my daughter in all her sixteen-year-old glory and I know it's impossible. *(Suddenly embarrassed.)* God, this conversation is so embarrassing.

ROWENA. No, it's not. It's real, honey...very real.

Beat.

What're you going to do?

PAM. Don't know. I'm scared. And angry.

ROWENA. The kids pick up on any of this?

PAM. I don't know. Maybe. They haven't said anything.

ROWENA. Well, don't do anything rash, girl. Keep your head. Think this thing through.

PAM. I know. But, Bernard's got to help. I'm not going to pull all the weight by myself. There's only so much I'm willing to take.

ROWENA. Anything I can do?

PAM. You listened to me. That's enough.

Beat.

Keep this conversation in this room?

Lights.

Scene 9

Griggs is in his office when Bernard enters.

BERNARD. You wanted to see me, Sam?

GRIGGS. Bernard! Sit down, son.

Bernard sits. Griggs goes to a small bar.

Drink?

BERNARD. Not on the job. You know me.

GRIGGS. Well, I sure as hell feel like one.

Griggs pours himself a drink.

If I hadn't seen it with my own eyes, I wouldn't have believed it.

BERNARD. *(Big smile.)* I told you I wouldn't let you down.

GRIGGS. The Arbitron numbers have been astronomical. To jump those many points in so short a time. And the letters I get. My God. The board is really proud of you, Bernard. But no more than me.

BERNARD. Thanks, Sam.

GRIGGS. I know we've had our differences in the past; you've always been so headstrong about things, but through it all I've always been able to count on you. That's not easy for a man like me.

BERNARD. We make a good team, Sam.

GRIGGS. A fine team, yes, indeed.

BERNARD. We still have a ways to go, yet. There're still some areas I need to fine-tune.

GRIGGS. That won't be necessary, just yet.

BERNARD. But, we need to keep pushing.

GRIGGS. That's why I had you come to my office, Bernard. Some things have come up.

BERNARD. Things?

GRIGGS. Well, our success has attracted a lot of attention.

BERNARD. I know. Our ad rates are climbing at all six of our stations.

GRIGGS. That's not what I mean, kid.

BERNARD. What do you mean?

GRIGGS. I've been approached by some people who want to buy my company.

BERNARD. Who?

GRIGGS. Pegasus International.

BERNARD. Are you going to do it?

GRIGGS. Right now, all I'm doing is listening to their offer. Nothing more.

BERNARD. I don't think it's a good idea, no matter how much they're offering.

GRIGGS. It doesn't hurt to know what I'm worth on today's market, now, does it?

BERNARD. I wish you had talked to me before you made your move.

GRIGGS. Listen, I want you to see to it that our stations maintain their current ratings. Keep our listeners and advertisers happy. Don't get cute. I want my operations functional and running smoothly.

BERNARD. Wow, Sam…I feel like you're asking me to be nothing more than a caretaker.

GRIGGS. I only want to make the best impression I can.

BERNARD. I finally get things turned around and you hit me with this?

GRIGGS. Now, don't be getting dramatic on me, kid…

BERNARD. Dramatic? Sam…I been with you fifteen years… I've had good offers to go elsewhere…but, I chose to stay…

GRIGGS. I know that, and I appreciate your loyalty, Bernard…

BERNARD. I mean, I knew with your not having any children to pass the business on to… Well, I figured, in time, if I was loyal enough…if I worked hard enough, I'd earn the right to expect… I mean, Sam, I learned everything from you. I was your right hand!

GRIGGS. Hang with me on this, kid. You won't be sorry.

Griggs presses his intercom.

Mary, have Al bring the car around.

BERNARD. You can make a lot more money holding on to Griggs Broadcasting than by selling it.

GRIGGS. Who said anything about selling? I haven't made up my mind to do anything.

BERNARD. You seem pretty damned close to me, Sam.

GRIGGS. Well, I'm not. Stop jumping to conclusions and do as I ask.

BERNARD. But, Sam…

GRIGGS. *(Impatient; guilty.)* Whatever move I make, you'll be the first to know. Now, I'll see you later. I've got to do this lunch.

Lights.

Scene 10

Lights come up full to reveal Pam, Marvin, Rowena, and Ron in evening gowns and black tie. We can hear music and voices in the background. They are at an alumni affair and sing the Howard University alma mater.

ALL. *(Singing.)*
Reared against the eastern sky
Proudly there on hilltop high
Far above the lake so blue
Stands old Howard firm and true.
There she stands for truth and right,
Sending forth her rays of light.
Clad in robes of majesty
   They raise white handkerchiefs and wave them.
Oh, Howard, we sing of thee.
   Lots of laughter, cheers, and applause.

ROWENA. Oh, how I hate coming to these things.

PAM. Oh, Rowena, you need to stop.

ROWENA. Everyone looking to see how fat everyone's gotten. Awful. *(Waves offstage.)* Oh, hi, Lois! *(Under her breath.)* Bitch.

MARVIN. Careful, baby, don't let her hear you.

ROWENA. I don't care. Never could stand that heifer.

   Bernard enters in a tux, carrying two wineglasses.

BERNARD. *(Gives one glass to Pam.)* Here you go, honey.

PAM. Wondered where you were. You took so long.

BERNARD. Ran into Harvey Benton at the bar.

MARVIN. Bubbleheaded Harvey?

BERNARD. The same.

MARVIN. Man, that guy had the biggest head I ever saw in my life.

BERNARD. He's still got it.

   They laugh.

ROWENA. You know Harvey and Charyce are getting a divorce, don't you?

MARVIN. Finally got tired of his mess, huh?

ROWENA. Guess so.

PAM. They got married the same day we did, honey.

BERNARD. Really.

PAM. Poor Charyce.

BERNARD. Poor Harvey...literally. That woman is going to take him to the cleaners.

ROWENA. I won't even dignify that remark with a reply.

PAM. I knew they were drifting apart. Charyce mentioned it to me, once or twice.

ROWENA. Sign of the times.

PAM. *(To Bernard.)* Harvey never said anything to you?

BERNARD. No, but I can't blame him.

ROWENA. Oh? Why not?

BERNARD. We work in the same business. You never give a competitor an edge against you, even if he is your friend.

ROWENA. This isn't about business. This is something personal.

BERNARD. Personal...or professional, it doesn't matter. If it's a weakness, it's exploitable.

PAM. Charyce and Harvey are friends. I don't see them as competitors.

BERNARD. Alright, maybe it's a male thing; a rule of the pack. I don't know. But, it exists.

PAM. You men should talk to Harvey.

BERNARD. When Harvey wants help, he'll let us know.

RON. Besides, there're at least twenty lawyers in this room. Harvey needs to talk to them more than he needs to talk to us.

The men laugh.

PAM. That's disgusting.

ROWENA. We should have brought our children. They need to see something like this. There must be close to one hundred million dollars' worth of black people in this room and none of them had to sell drugs, rob, steal, or knock somebody over the head to get that money, either.

RON. You really think there's that much, Ro?

ROWENA. Well...fifty.

RON. Hmmm. Excuse me.

MARVIN. Wait up, Ron.

Both men wander off, business cards at the ready, intent on "networking."

ROWENA. I'm thinking about putting my girls in the Jack and Jills.

BERNARD. What?

ROWENA. You heard me, Bernard. You ain't deaf.

PAM. I think it's a wonderful idea. Young girls today need the kind of shaping Jack and Jill can give them.

ROWENA. Don't I know it.

PAM. And what do your daughters think?

ROWENA. They don't want to join, naturally.

PAM. All girls are like that. It's something new and that's one thing teenagers hate: the new and unknown.

ROWENA. Tell me about it.

BERNARD. You oughta be putting those girls in a computer camp or getting them in the Jaycees, or something. Teach them about power and how it shapes people's lives. Need to teach those girls something real.

PAM. Oh, Bernard.

BERNARD. And what made you decide to put your daughters in the Jack and Jill, anyway?

ROWENA. This little rogue my big girl brought home. Little tack-head thing, with twenty-two gold teeth cloggin' up his mouth and his hands stuck all down his pockets and this little hat titched on the side of his head like it was growin' out of his temple, or somethin'.

BERNARD. *(Laughs.)* "Mama, this is Bubba, and I *love* him."

ROWENA. How'd you know? That's *exactly* what she said.

43

Bernard laughs harder.

It ain't funny. Here me and Marvin are bustin' our butts making all this money to send our kids to the best private schools and buy them the nicest clothes, tryin' to give them the best life has to offer, and what happens? She goes out and brings me a "Bubba" with a mouth fulla more gold than Fort Knox.

BERNARD. Relax. It's just an infatuation. She'll get over it.

ROWENA. For all I know that boy could be one of those drive-by shooters they talk about on TV.

BERNARD. You talk just like one of those middle-class biddies I used to hate when I was a kid.

ROWENA. Well, I *am* a middle-class biddie, Bernard. And I'm putting my daughter in the Jack and Jills where she might have a chance to meet some nice young boy who's going to go to college and make something of himself.

BERNARD. And the first thing he'll make is your daughter. While you're so busy watching that tackhead, it's that little slickhead in the tuxedo who's got your daughter in the backseat of his daddy's BMW on cotillion night.

PAM. Don't listen to him, Ro. The Jack and Jills are wonderful. I was in the Jack and Jills and I loved every minute of it.

BERNARD. I can remember a time when we wouldn't have been caught dead at a Jack and Jill ball, and now here we are talking about putting one of our children in one.

PAM. We've grown up, thank God.

Beat.

Getting older.

ROWENA. Speak for yourself, Pamela.

PAM. I don't mind, really. Each new birthday brings on something new and exciting. I don't want to be twenty again. Today's kids have too many problems.

BERNARD. The times are different. In our day we had heroes who told us we could grab fate and shake its tail. King, Malcolm, the Kennedys—

ROWENA. Ella Baker, Fannie Lou Hamer.

BERNARD. *(Agreeing.)* Teach. Well, they're all dead, now. And no one's risen to take their places. We came of age in a time when no dream was impossible, and no affliction was so terrible, it couldn't be overcome. Remember?

ROWENA. But, it wasn't really like that.

BERNARD. We believed in something, then. What do kids believe in, today? Instead, everyone is just out here trying to survive.

PAM. Why dwell on it, Bernard? You can't change anything.

BERNARD. Yea, you're right, Pam. You've always had a level head about these things.

> *Bernard and Pam exchange glances. Marvin sees this and speaks up quickly.*

MARVIN. Come on, let's change the subject and talk about something real.

ROWENA. Okay, let's. Who wants to start?

> *Silence.*

Let's not all speak at once.

RON. I want some more champagne. That's real. Anybody else?

> *Ron starts off.*

BERNARD. Let's talk about fidelity...or infidelity.

> *Ron stops.*

PAM. What? Why?

BERNARD. Because it's *real*.

RON. I don't know, man.

ROWENA. Who wants to talk about that? We all get along fine.

BERNARD. Well, so did Harvey and Charyce.

PAM. They fell out of love. You need love in a relationship.

BERNARD. That what happened with you and Irene, Ron? Y'all stopped loving each other?

RON. That was a long time ago.

ROWENA. All you need is love, Bernard. Strongest glue there is.

BERNARD. Is it? How many times can one's love stand being tested? How many years of making love the same old way; how many days of the same kinds of conversations; how many nights of sleeping on the same side of the bed, having the same old dreams. Huh?

PAM. If you really love someone, Bernard, that kind of stuff doesn't happen.

BERNARD. I had an uncle who carried on an affair with a woman for some twenty years. All the time he was married. My aunt had six children for him. The other lady had three. He swore he loved both women. Was he lyin'? Was he bored with his life and didn't want to face it? What? Why does a man do something like that?

ROWENA. Suppose you'll tell us.

BERNARD. I think one day my uncle looked up and saw he was living his life by everyone's expectations except his own. He was scared he had lost himself and one day he broke out by having an affair with another woman.

PAM. Well, things like that can happen sometimes, but it doesn't mean it's right.

RON. Sometimes, when a man is a failure in one part of his life, he tries to become a success in another. What was he—an ordinary laborer, or something?

BERNARD. *(Testy.)* He had money, Ron.

MARVIN. Come on, Bernard, he only meant—

BERNARD. I *know* what he meant. My uncle had his own business. Owned a house. Got himself a new car every two or three years. Sent all his kids off to school, too. Loved and respected by his neighbors and the folks at church. So, what happened? What made him break like that?

RON. Biological determinism.

BERNARD. What?

MARVIN. He's saying your uncle was acting out a primal instinct that resides in every human male.

ROWENA. It better not reside in *you*. I do know *that*.

MARVIN. Course not, baby.

ROWENA. Biological determinism. You men will come up with any kind of excuse to camouflage your lack of sexual discipline.

MARVIN. Discipline? I didn't know you were into freaky deaky, baby.

All laugh, except Bernard.

ROWENA. *(Playfully.)* Marvin, hush.

They laugh again. Bernard looks at them.

BERNARD. We're getting off the subject.

RON. What is the subject?

Bernard looks at him.

Oh, yes. Infidelity.

BERNARD. It goes beyond infidelity. Look, I'm trying to get at something, here. I feel like we're in a lot of trouble.

RON. I think the brother's had a little too much to drink.

BERNARD. I'm *fine.*

RON. Then what is the something you're trying to get at? You've been running your mouth all night. Why don't you get down to it?

Bernard glares at Ron and suddenly blurts out:

BERNARD. Fuck you, man. *Fuck* you!

RON. *(Tense.)* I think the brother's had too much to drink.

Bernard starts for Ron. Marvin gets between them.

MARVIN. Hey, man! Bernard! This is us, remember?

Bernard struggles, but Marvin holds him fast.

Remember?!

RON. Excuse me.

Rowena goes after Ron. Marvin soon follows. Bernard moves downstage in another direction. Pam moves toward him.

BERNARD. Doesn't it ever bother you, Pam? Doesn't it ever get on your nerves? We're so full of shit.

Lights.

Scene 11

Bernard stands alone in a spot.

BERNARD. I knew something was wrong when I began to hate them. It went against everything I had ever come to believe in. People whom I had once viewed as the victims of everything that was wrong with America; the perfect human metaphors for our society's very real failures, now stood before me, an endless parade of poor downtrodden men holding squeegees in their hands, fighting each other over the privilege of wiping my windshield for fifty cents.

What would Du Bois have thought if he could see what the last days of the twentieth century had brought to black people? What would Douglass or Garvey have thought? The sons and daughters of Africa; the descendants of the survivors of the middle passage—the heartiest black people who ever lived—now reduced to standing on street corners selling their bodies for a drug fix and clubbing each other with broom handles for the right to make a couple of quarters washing someone's windshield.

Instead of lamenting their sorry fate, I hated them because I knew there was nothing I could do to change their lives. They would always be there, day after horrible day. Their lives would never change. I had managed to grab the brass ring and I was being pulled up and away from them, floating higher and higher. I would survive the madness and they would not. And I hated them for not surviving, for ensuring that the intelligence they had, the love they were once capable of giving, were to be denied to our people. I came to see that the legacy bequeathed them by the many thousands gone, by all the blood that was shed, had truly been wasted on them. There was no help for them. And I hated them for making me realize that I had to abandon them lest I be pulled down with them.

And that's when I realized that something was wrong. Who gave me the right to judge them? Who gave me the right to feel superior? I act as though there is nothing I can do. But, that can't be true. It just can't be.

Lights.

Scene 12

Lights up on Bernard and Griggs standing on the promontory at Eagle Rock Reservation.

GRIGGS. I love coming up here.

BERNARD. You used to bring me up here when I first started working for you.

He looks at Griggs. He knows something is up.

GRIGGS. You can see all the way to New York. Must be a good twenty miles.

BERNARD. Fourteen. Remember?

GRIGGS. Yes, fourteen. Of course.

Bernard looks at Griggs.

BERNARD. Why're we up here, Sam?

GRIGGS. Don't want to beat around the bush. Good. You see, I wanted a place where we could really talk. Away from the office. I wanted to explain to you—

BERNARD. You're going to sell to Pegasus.

GRIGGS. Yes.

BERNARD. Then, there's nothing to talk about.

GRIGGS. There's plenty to talk about.

BERNARD. Hey, man, it's your station. You do what you want.

GRIGGS. Don't you take that tone with me.

BERNARD. Why don't you give me some time, Sam? I know I can come up with the backing to make you a very fair offer.

GRIGGS. Bernard, what have our grosses been? In our *best* year? Ten, twelve million? These guys pull down those kinds of bucks in a month! That's the kind of world we live in, now. You can't compete in a world like that, nickel-and-diming your way along.

BERNARD. I know how to compete in that world, Sam. I've spent a career wading through that world helping you build this company. I didn't do it with mirrors.

GRIGGS. *(Sighs.)* Sorry, Bernard. My mind's made up. I've made provisions for you to stay on. They're going to move you over to their facilities in Fort Lee. Our offices are slated to be torn down and the land cleared for sale.

BERNARD. And you expect me to work for these people?

>   *Pause.*

GRIGGS. They're very impressed with that Urban Cutting Edge Format you've developed. They want you to run things for them during the interim. Of course, one of their guys will be in overall charge, but you know how that is.

BERNARD. Sam, I can't believe this, man.

GRIGGS. They'll want you to diminish that controversial stuff. Politics and black radio don't mix. They'll want you to keep it light. "Infotainment." I think that's the phrase they used.

BERNARD. Dammit, Sam, you had no right to do this. It's my turn. This is *my* shot.

GRIGGS. Make your own shot, goddammit! Like I had to!

BERNARD. And that's the justification?! You had a hard time, so every young person who comes after you has to do the same? How do we develop an economic base for our people if we keep selling off our businesses in the name of fiscal expediency? How do we encourage our young kids if we block them at every turn and leave them with no institutions to take over after we've gone? Answer me that, Sam?

GRIGGS. There it is: that same smarmy, baby-boom self-righteousness I've had to put up with for the past twenty goddamn years! I'm not going to be judged by your expectations, or anyone else's. I'm doing what I think is right!

BERNARD. The black community was changing, Sam! It was up to us to be at the forefront of that change!

GRIGGS. It was too dangerous!

BERNARD. But, that was our job, Sam! There were new voices and ideas out there that needed to be heard. Poets and musicians who might've been able to give our people something more than twenty-four hours of "Ow, ow, ow! Give it to me, Mama, while you shake your thang!" It's never been your station to do as you please, Sam.

It belongs to the people. It should have been their voice. Not their sleeping pill.

GRIGGS. Well, I remember things differently, Bernard. Every time something jumped off at the studio I had the FBI, the FCC, and the local police hanging around the station with subpoenas, search warrants, questionnaires, and who knows what else. Every time some militant ran off at the mouth, or some singer warbled a lyric that some scared bureaucrat construed to be a call for black people to riot in the streets. I wasn't going to have that. I wasn't going to have my business go down the tubes on a bullshit tip! Hell, no!

BERNARD. I used to hear dudes lecture about you in school, man. Your name was right up there with Walker, Fuller, Johnson...Lewis and Smith—all the pioneers in black business. I never thought I'd live to see the day when you'd become content to be just another anonymous business transaction on some white man's ledger.

GRIGGS. Look, they're going to be paying you a lot of money. More than I ever paid you. And let me remind you, "Mr. Guardian of the Great Black Consciousness," that the most revolutionary, political act any black man can perform in this country is to successfully take care of his family—because *no one expects him to!*

> Beat.

Look, maybe one day you'll get a chance to do your own thing. But, not right now. This ain't the first time a black man has had to wait his turn. Take the job, Bernard. Go with these guys. Everybody else is.

> Bernard turns his back and begins walking away.

So, what's it going to be? You going to be a righteous revolutionary with no prospects, or a pragmatic businessman who looked the dragon in the eye...and decided to wear an asbestos suit? I want an answer soon, and it better be the right one.

Scene 13

Pam and Bernard at home.

PAM. You know, we've got money saved and I'm working.

BERNARD. I know.

PAM. How could they fire you like that? No warning. Nothing. Just fired.

BERNARD. I had warnings.

PAM. *(Looks at him.)* Then, you should have heeded them.

BERNARD. I wasn't going to keep letting those people get on my nerves. Me and Griggs had words. I told him what I thought of his policies and he fired me.

PAM. Well, you know how hot-tempered Griggs is. Go back and talk to him. See if you can get your job back.

BERNARD. Maybe I don't want it back.

PAM. You think that's wise? You need a job, honey.

BERNARD. Right. A job. Not *that* job.

PAM. What are you going to do?

BERNARD. I want to go after Griggs Broadcasting.

PAM. Go after it? You mean buy it?

BERNARD. Yes. It won't be easy. But, I know I can raise the money.

PAM. It takes time to make something like that work.

BERNARD. Griggs'll stall Pegasus, trying to drive the price up. If he waits long enough, that just might give me the time I need.

PAM. That's the future. What about now?

BERNARD. I'll find something.

PAM. You'd be putting quite a strain on yourself. Working full time, plus trying to raise money—

BERNARD. I don't see that I have any other choice.

PAM. Yes, you do. You could try to talk to Griggs.

BERNARD. Too late for that. I want more, now.

PAM. Griggs has already made up his mind. You can't win that fight.

BERNARD. I've got to try.

PAM. If we were in our twenties or early thirties, I might be inclined to say go for it. The children were small, then, but those days are over. You're almost forty-five years old. It's time you put your feet firmly on the ground. We have responsibilities—

BERNARD. You want me to give up?

PAM. I want you to be practical.

BERNARD. *Fuck* being practical, goddammit! Look what being practical for the past twenty years has gotten me!

PAM. Cursing at me is not going to change the reality of the situation, Bernard.

BERNARD. Oh, Pam, I'm not raising my voice at you. It's just that, for the past few months I've felt things closing in on me. Alarm bells are going off inside my head all the time: "Make your move, now, Bernard. Make your move, now."

PAM. Why is it you only see what you haven't accomplished, and completely ignore the good things you've done with your life?

BERNARD. Because I know I'm supposed to be further down the road. That's why.

PAM. I love you, Bernard. But, if you're going to allow everything we've spent all these years building up to come crashing down around our heads, I'll fight you. I swear before God I will fight you tooth and nail.

She turns and goes out. Bernard remains onstage.

Scene 14

A golf course in Essex County, New Jersey. Pam, Bernard, Ron, Marvin, and Rowena on the links. Pam is first off the tee.

ROWENA. Oh, Pam. Great shot!

PAM. Best I've ever done, I think.

MARVIN. Sliced it too much, if you ask me.

ROWENA. No one did, so hush. You men are always so critical.

RON. Come on, Ro. Your turn.

> *Rowena steps up to the tee. Marvin looks at Bernard.*

MARVIN. Come on, man. Get in the game.

BERNARD. Got my mind on other things.

RON. Better concentrate on this game, bro. The sistuhs are serious about beatin' us, this time.

ROWENA. Damned right.

> *Whack! Rowena's shot flies off the tee. Everyone except Bernard oohs and aahs.*

PAM. Bernard? Your turn, honey.

BERNARD. I need to talk to y'all.

> *He steps to the tee, places his ball down.*

MARVIN. Yeah, well, talk while you're playing, bro. That's what golf's all about.

> *Bernard takes his time setting himself and lining up his shot.*

BERNARD. I'm organizing a counterbid to acquire Griggs Broadcasting. I need y'all to put your money where your friendship is.

> *Bernard drives a tremendous tee shot.*

MARVIN. Damn!

BERNARD. Is that a comment on my statement, or my shot?

ROWENA. *(Under her breath.)* Both.

PAM. Honey, I thought you were going to think this thing through before you discussed it with anybody?

BERNARD. I have thought it through. What do y'all think?

ROWENA. Well…uh…it sounds interesting…

MARVIN. *(Steps to the tee.)* Kind of caught me off guard, Bernard, I mean, hey, I'm playing golf, man.

BERNARD. This is the right move at the right time. Communications is a growth industry. We could—

RON. You don't have to sell us on the virtues of the broadcast business, brother.

MARVIN. That's quite a lot of money you've got to raise, my man.

BERNARD. I've got the will and the expertise, and y'all have got the kinds of contacts I'd need to get things moving. What do you say?

Whack! Rowena drives her shot.

ROWENA. I like the idea.

PAM. We could organize a dinner party, invite some key people, and get the ball rolling. I can have my office put the prospectus together in no time.

MARVIN. A limited partnership would be enticing...

BERNARD. Then, it's agreed. You'll do it.

All except Ron chime in words of agreement. Ron looks at them all. Then:

RON. No.

BERNARD. What?

RON. Sorry, Bernard, I think it's a bad move.

ROWENA. You're wrong.

RON. Think on it: The growth area in communications is not radio. It's cable TV.

BERNARD. Hey, look, I'm the one who has a communications background, not you.

Ron steps to the tee. As he speaks he places his ball, sets himself and lines up his shot. Occasionally, he allows himself to make direct eye contact with Bernard.

RON. Then use that knowledge to look ahead. Find a cable franchise that's on the block, then talk to us. Just looking out for your interest, brother. You gotta put your money where it'll do the most good.

ROWENA. Maybe Ron is right.

PAM. I don't know. Maybe Bernard is right. Ron could be wrong about this.

Ron swings. Whack!

RON. It's unlikely. The think tank at my company did some comparative studies, and—

BERNARD. Tell me something, Ron. You ever hear of people taking their portable cable TV to the beach with them? Does cable TV ride around with them in their cars, or go with them when they're out jogging? Or shopping? Or picnicking? Or doing *anything* outside of the house? Radio is *always* there. Instant communication. Instant information. Touching base with our people whenever and wherever. That's what radio offers. That's why it will always be an important component to people's lives. And that's what makes it a sound investment. You sit around listening to some slick Ivy League bean counters running their mouths over some fancy food in a Wall Street restaurant and suddenly you want to stand out here and pontificate as if you have insight into the Great Secrets of Life. I *know* what I'm talking about. I'm not a fool.

RON. Nobody said you were, brother.

BERNARD. Then, shut the hell up, goddammit and stay outa my way!

> *Bernard moves away. His outburst has made everyone uneasy. Pause.*

How about the rest of y'all?

ROWENA. I'm sorry, Bernard. But Ron's still given me some food for thought. But, let me see a prospectus.

BERNARD. Sure, and you'll get back to me. Right?

MARVIN. Uh…er…it's starting to cloud up. Let's get a few more holes in before it rains.

ROWENA. Yes, let's go.

> *Marvin and Rowena move on. Pam and Ron linger with Bernard.*

RON. Sorry, Bernard. I wasn't out to hurt your feelings, or anything. I just felt I had to speak my mind.

BERNARD. Your kind of thinking calls itself being careful and prudent, but it's really just a disguise for a lack of vision and the willingness to ACT. I'm going to get Griggs Broadcasting, Ron. I won't let men like you get in my way ever again.

> *Ron and Bernard stare each other down. Then:*

RON. Better watch this next hole, brother. There's a helluva sand trap.

> *Bernard says nothing as Ron moves off and Pam moves close to him.*
>
> *Lights.*

Scene 15

The next afternoon. Bernard and Tanya, in Tanya's apartment.

BERNARD. Just talk to your friends, and have them talk to some of their friends. We'll call a meeting and I'll have a prospectus for them to look at.

TANYA. Bernard, my friends are a pretty conservative bunch. We're very careful at what we do.

BERNARD. You know anything about Pegasus International?

TANYA. They're an up-and-coming communications conglomerate. Not nearly as big as their name implies.

BERNARD. Which means they can be defeated. We're not talking a transcontinental megacorp here.

TANYA. My people'll want a sure thing.

BERNARD. Then, they're crazy. There *are* no sure things in life.

TANYA. The history of our people is filled with dreamers and impulsive people like you. The list of their failures is long.

BERNARD. Then, help me write some new history, Tanya.

TANYA. And what does your wife think?

BERNARD. What do you care about what my wife thinks?

TANYA. Just curious.

BERNARD. Don't play games with me, Tanya.

TANYA. No need to get upset. I just asked a question.

BERNARD. This some kind of litmus test? Give you the wrong answer and you won't help.

TANYA. Did I say that?

BERNARD. It's hard to tell. Women start getting notions in their heads and they stop speaking English. Suddenly, they're speaking metaphors and subtleties.

TANYA. What is it with you?

BERNARD. I'm just tired of bullshit, Tanya. Okay?

TANYA. No, it's not okay. I'm the one on the emotional limb, Bernard.

I'm the one who only gets pieces of you, while she enjoys all of you. I'm the one alone on the holidays, I'm the one who remains in the shadows. I'm the one who soothes you and quiets you after she's put you down and hurt you. I think I have a right to ask questions and a right to some answers. You always want my help, but what do I ever receive in return?

BERNARD. Maybe you're right.

TANYA. I know I'm right. Now, what does your wife think?

BERNARD. She thinks I should get my old job back.

TANYA. And you really believe you can outbid Griggs Broadcasting?

BERNARD. Help me, and I'll show you.

TANYA. I'll do whatever I can. I love you, Bernard. I love you.

> *They kiss. Bernard goes into the other room. Tanya goes to a telephone and dials. She holds the receiver to her ear a moment, then, as it is still ringing, she hangs the phone up and walks away.*

Scene 16

Pam and Rowena in the sauna.

ROWENA. Mmmmm, this feels so good.

> *Pam says nothing.*

So…uh…you find out who the broad is, yet?

PAM. No. I'm not sure I want to.

ROWENA. If it was me, I'd just have to know.

PAM. The fact that he's seeing someone is painful enough without having to know who the woman is.

ROWENA. So, what are you going to do about it?

PAM. I don't know, yet. I mean, I'm not sure.

ROWENA. You're sure.

PAM. I don't understand why he feels the need. What did I do?

ROWENA. Find you somebody.

PAM. I'm not interested in finding somebody.

ROWENA. Get interested.

PAM. I don't want to.

ROWENA. It'll dry up if you don't use it, girl.

PAM. Maybe I should have told him how I felt. Maybe if I had been more giving…more open.

ROWENA. Confront him.

PAM. No. I mean, not yet.

ROWENA. Well, if this marriage is important to you, don't waste time.

PAM. I won't. Don't worry.

> *Beat.*

Hmph. "The Perfect Couple."

ROWENA. What?

PAM. That's what *Jet* magazine said when we got married; the Perfect Couple.

ROWENA. I remember.

PAM. I didn't like that article. Didn't like us being called that. Bad luck.

ROWENA. Shoot, it was perfect: the daughter of a traditional, old-line black Southern family with money getting married to a new-generation black militant whose work even white critics liked. It knocked us all out when we first heard it.

PAM. You know, my parents didn't want me to marry him.

ROWENA. You never told me that.

PAM. Well, it's true.

ROWENA. Why?

PAM. I don't want to talk about it.

ROWENA. It wasn't because your folks didn't want no big, black-skinned Negro sleeping with their light-skinned daughter, was it?

PAM. *(Sharply.)* No, that wasn't it, at all.

ROWENA. I thought so.

PAM. Well, you're wrong.

ROWENA. Sure.

Beat.

PAM. I never thought I would be right for him. You knew me back in those days. I wasn't militant enough for the kind of people you and Bernard used to hang out with. I didn't particularly go for wearing all those African clothes. It seemed so phony. They just weren't practical for use in a Western society. I mean, I'm African descended, but I'm not an African.

Rowena looks at her, then looks away.

ROWENA. You weren't supposed to get him, you know. Habiba was.

PAM. Oh, yes. Bessie Johnson. The zoology major. If Bernard was serious about her, he would have let me know.

ROWENA. Well, you were considered one of the most attractive girls on campus. All the men had their eyes on you.

PAM. I used to catch hell for not being black enough. What did that mean? I was as black as any of them.

ROWENA. It wasn't about ethnicity. It was about where your mind was at.

PAM. Well, I am the way I am. I'm not changing for anybody. All that African stuff and hardly any of them understood what it all meant. They were always so right—or "righteous." And I was always so wrong. Everything about me was wrong. I was too smart…too Western…too middle class…too pretty…

ROWENA. Too light?

PAM. What's my color got to do with it?

ROWENA. It helped you beat out Habiba.

PAM. My color is not my fault.

ROWENA. A lot of people felt you thought it was a great advantage.

PAM. Is that how you felt?

ROWENA. I always felt it was a great burden.

PAM. I'm not sure I know how to take that.

ROWENA. Think about it, honey.

Beat.

PAM. Ro, you really think he married me because of the color of my skin. *(Looks away.)* This is the kind of thing that can drive you crazy. Suddenly, you start questioning everything.

ROWENA. Don't drive yourself crazy, girl.

PAM. I caught hell from your old group because I was light-skinned, didn't I?

ROWENA. No, I wouldn't say that.

PAM. I would.

ROWENA. Look, Claudia Truitt was as light as you and she didn't have any problem with us.

PAM. Claudia Truitt had a large flat nose, full lips, and a big behind. There was never any mistake about her. We all know I'm not like that.

> Pause.

His color attracted me, you know. There was something so warm and sensuous about him. There were times when he positively glistened.

ROWENA. He still does, from time to time.

PAM. I wanted that warmth.

ROWENA. Who didn't?

PAM. I knew I had to have him. And winning him from all you "relevant" and "righteous" campus militants felt so good.

ROWENA. Really.

PAM. It was a question of class, too, Rowena. A street boy going to college. All my life I had been shielded from men like him. And now here was one up close. I loved it.

ROWENA. A less sympathetic ear might accuse you of slumming.

PAM. I never felt that way.

ROWENA. You never had to. You stood to benefit from the rules of the game, whether you wanted to or not. It's crazy. We were supposed to have buried this color thing a long time ago. Look, can we change the subject?

PAM. We were just deluding ourselves.

> Beat.

I have a dark-skinned cousin who lives in Newark, not even twenty minutes from here. She hates the sight of me. Won't even speak to me. Hates all light-skinned people…and never lets me forget it. It's all part of something that's been going on in my family since before I was born… I've always been afraid that, somewhere deep in his heart, Bernard hates me.

ROWENA. Hates you?

PAM. Yes. Maybe it was some perverse self-hatred that made him marry me and now, years later, it's starting to surface; he can't suppress it any longer.

ROWENA. Bernard oughta be horsewhipped for what he's doing to you.

PAM. Did you love him?

ROWENA. Who?

PAM. Bernard.

ROWENA. Bernard?

PAM. Yes. At Howard. Did you love him?

ROWENA. Ah…I-I-I-I-I…

PAM. Well, did you?

ROWENA. Yes, but only in the political sense.

PAM. And you hated me for getting him, didn't you?

ROWENA. What are you talking about? Habiba had him.

PAM. And you all really loved Habiba. Big-butt, dark-skinned, African-looking Habiba. She was one of *you*.

ROWENA. Pam—

PAM. And you hated me and you *still* hate me.

ROWENA. No more, alright?

PAM. Oh, I've always known how you've felt about me.

ROWENA. Will you stop?

PAM. Habiba was part of your little crowd: that tight little dark-skinned women's collective you all had. I moved in and snapped my tapioca fingers and y'all's ebony idol was scooped up, just like that.

ROWENA. Now, just a minute!

PAM. I'm just laying my cards on the table, Ro.

ROWENA. Shit! You act like the pain doesn't cut both ways. "Dark-skinned women's collective"? Why do you think that was? Huh?! "Well, honey, you so dark you sure can't be pretty. You'd better be smart." Straightening combs dug so deep down into your scalp till the pain made your eyes water. All from trying to make the hair do something it wasn't meant to do and had no business even trying. Excluded from certain circles; not invited to certain parties. Always waiting to be chosen after y—

She doesn't finish the sentence.

There were always reasons for "dark-skinned women's collectives," Pam. I can still remember a mural on the wall of a restaurant across the street from the campus. It showed campus life back in the thirties, or whenever it was painted. All the students in the mural looked like you, Pam; none of them looked like me.

Yes, I was angry when you took Bernard. It seemed like a confirmation of every feeling of inferiority that had hounded me since birth.

PAM. I can't help the way I look. There are white people in Richmond with the same family name as mine. Some of them look just like my aunts and uncles. They know who I am. They know my whole family. And yet, when we walk down the street and they see us coming they look the other way like we're not even there. Every year when I take the children down home, all the old folks trip over themselves to see who gets to check my children's hair first. How do you think that makes me feel? And right there in Newark, just twenty minutes away, I've got a black cousin the same age as me with two children I have never seen and she treats me like shit!

ROWENA. I've spent most of the last twenty years trying to put all the pain aside.

PAM. Nothing's working out, Ro. It's like all my life has been one right move after the other and now, suddenly, everything is being thrown back in my face and I don't even know why. I'm tired of being the yella bitch and I'm tired of being the tragic mulatto. I hate what whites have done to my family and I hate what my family has done to itself. And I hate what they have ALL done to me.

ROWENA. What about what you've done to yourself?

PAM. Sometimes I hurt so bad. I just hurt.

ROWENA. All black women carry scars, Pam.

PAM. They never go away.

ROWENA. We'll never be able to do anything about the pain others cause us until we do something about the pain we're causing ourself.

> *Pam says nothing. The women sit in silence…and quietly reach out to one another.*

Scene 17

> *A week later, Bernard, Ron, and Marvin at their favorite bar.*

BERNARD and MARVIN. Africa?!

RON. Why not? The chance of a lifetime.

MARVIN. You just gonna pack up everything and move over there?

RON. I'm already taking a Berlitz course in Swahili, brother.

BERNARD. Surprised me, man. I never would've expected it of you.

RON. Well, you ought to know me by now, Bernard. I'm full of surprises.

BERNARD. Anyway, I think it's a great idea.

MARVIN. Yea. *You* would.

BERNARD. I was in Africa, once.

MARVIN. Yea, we know: Angola.

BERNARD. It's beautiful, man. You'll love it.

RON. Angola's communist, man. I can't make no money there.

MARVIN. Ron, you know they got that tribalism thing in Africa, man. Everything's fine as long as you hooked up with the right tribe. But, hey, that could all change any minute.

RON. Don't worry. I got it under control.

BERNARD. Kwame hooked this all up?

RON. Told you contacting him would pay off, one day.

BERNARD. Damn.

RON. He's up there in the minister of agriculture's office. I'll be livin' out in the bush, man. My own spread, a staff—the works.

Bernard raises his glass to toast Ron. Marvin does, also.

MARVIN. Looks like you're going to be a pioneer.

RON. And a rich one to boot. I make this irrigation idea of mine work, I'll patent it and market it all over the Continent.

BERNARD. Could be quite a boost to the African economy.

RON. Hey, man, I look like UNESCO to you?

MARVIN. I just hope you'll be careful, Ron. I mean, you're going to be a long way from home and well, this is the first time you've seen Kwame since our college days, man. Who knows how much he's changed.

RON. Not that much. He's ambitious as ever. He's going to run for office.

BERNARD and MARVIN. Kwame?!

RON. He'll win, too. He's very popular. He's got six wives, man.

MARVIN. Damn, you know *that* brother's in shape.

RON. Each from the most powerful villages in his region. So, you know he's got connections, and his father's a chief who sits in the national assembly.

MARVIN. Damn!

RON. Wide open, man. We could make the kind of moves our grandchildren won't even be able to dream about over here.

BERNARD. No wonder you became a Republican.

RON. Yea, well, the Republicans help those who help themselves, and I'm going to help myself to some of the Mother Country.

MARVIN. Like I said, man: Don't get in over your head.

RON. Look, I'm forty-one years old, going nowhere fast. Stuck in a middle-management position at my firm, with no prospects of a promotion. I trained two of the people who are now up for vice president.

MARVIN. Hey, man, there's a lot of us in that boat. It's not your fault. You can't help that.

RON. Yes, I can. I can get the hell outa there. I'm not going to spend the rest of my life being a circus animal—a feature on the sideshow of somebody else's main event. Africa's been making a whole lotta money for everybody else, time she made some for one of her prodigal sons.

BERNARD. Gotta tell you, man: You don't sound like the kind of son Mother Africa wants to see. If all you've got to offer her is one more rip-off mentality then what you need to do is keep your "prodigal" ass here.

RON. Later for you, man. I know what I'm doing.

BERNARD. That's what's so scary. And so sad.

RON. Sorry, man. I refuse to feel guilty about *not* feeling guilty. Know what I'm saying?

BERNARD. Yea. Cecil Rhodes would be real proud of you, Ron.

RON. Kiss my ass, Bernard. Why don't you take that sixties anger and stuff it.

BERNARD. Somebody oughta stuff *you*.

MARVIN. Fellas, this is starting to get a little thick. Why don't we just cool it and go on home?

RON. Good idea.

BERNARD. Y'all go ahead. I don't feel like going home.

MARVIN. I think you've had enough to drink for one night. Pam'll start to worry, man.

BERNARD. Maybe she will. Maybe she won't.

MARVIN. Hey, what's that supposed to mean?

BERNARD. If ya'll are going, go ahead.

RON. What's buggin' you, man?

BERNARD. I think me and Pam's had it, man.

MARVIN. It's that other broad you've been seeing. You're letting her get in the way, man. I told you to cut her loose.

BERNARD. It's all gonna come crashing down, man. Later for it. Whatever happens, happens. It's no use, anymore.

MARVIN. Bernard, are you drunk? What the hell are you talkin' about, man?

BERNARD. There's a point where the line between your professional life and your personal life blurs; where the choices you made in terms of one are a mirror reflection of the choices you made in the other. If you're an honest man and true to your heart and your beliefs, there's no problem. But, if not—

RON. I'm going home. I'll see y'all later.

MARVIN. Wait, don't leave, Ron.

RON. And he's got the nerve to talk about me. No, man, if he wants to act the fool, don't expect me to hang around and watch while he's doing it.

MARVIN. We're supposed to be friends. We should talk.

RON. He should talk to his wife and kids. They're the ones whose lives he's messin' up.

BERNARD. What would you have me do, Ron? Keep up the lies, keep on frontin' my game like everybody else around here?

RON. I don't have an answer for you, Bernard. But I will tell you this: This life we've got right now is all we've got. You understand? Don't ask me to give you advice on how to tear that life apart.

BERNARD. This life we've got is no life at all, Ron. It's a lie!

RON. Then lie to me, baby, 'cause I damn sure am enjoying the *hell* out of *this* untruth.

BERNARD. Thank God, I'm not. I'm tired of the lies. I'm tired of being a role model. I have no real wealth, no power, and, ultimately, no respect. And if that's the life I'm offering to my kids, then I'm damned well pleased to be "messing" it up.

RON. You make me nervous, Bernard. You ask too many questions. You push too hard. Always been your downfall. You need to learn to do like me, brother. I'm gonna go home, put some Coltrane on the box, sip some scotch, and then go to sleep and dream about Africa and a lot of money, and wake up tomorrow and know that all is right with the world.

> *Ron starts out.*

Don't be a fool, Bernard. Don't be a fool.

BERNARD. *(Looks at Marvin.)* That the way you feel, too? I'm a fool?

> *Marvin says nothing.*

Y'all just don't understand, man.

MARVIN. And Pam, does she understand?

BERNARD. No.

MARVIN. *(Takes a drink.)* I used to envy you.

BERNARD. I used to envy me, too.

MARVIN. I remember when ya'll hooked up in school. Couldn't figure out how a Papa Booga Bear like you managed to end up with the foxiest mama in the junior class.

BERNARD. She was as mysterious as Habiba was predictable.

MARVIN. Oh, yeah... *(Looks at Bernard.)* You need to forget about Habiba, Bernard. There's nothing you can do or say to her. She's been dead, for years.

BERNARD. If I only could have explained to her—

MARVIN. Look, she was the one who made the decision to go to Angola. You didn't have anything to do with that.

BERNARD. Angola was all me and her used to talk about. We took that liberating the Continent stuff seriously, man. Fighting for justice for black people wherever they are. All a that. We used to sit up till all hours talking about that.

MARVIN. I told the both of you, then, you were crazy. The Angolans could take care of themselves. The last thing in the world they needed was to have some starry-eyed young colored kids from the US running around over there getting in the way.

BERNARD. We didn't used to think like that.

MARVIN. Maybe that was our problem. Besides, what was Habiba gonna do for you with her five-year-old sandals, long no-shape-to-them dresses, hair braided-up, no make-up wearin' self?

BERNARD. You loved her, too. Remember?

MARVIN. Damned right, I loved her. Still do. But, she's dead...and so are the days she lived in.

BERNARD. If those days are dead, they're dead because we let them die.

MARVIN. They died because they had to.

BERNARD. I was a good writer. With a little polish I might have been a great one. Now, all I am is an out-of-work vice president of a radio station who's spent the past fifteen years selling dog food to people I once tried to move to political change.

MARVIN. Oh, boo-hoo, boo-hoo. I can see your tear-stained face driving your BMW all the way to the bank.

BERNARD. Sound like Pam.

MARVIN. That's because Pam's got a lot of sense. She knows you can't help the poor by being poor yourself.

BERNARD. I think that's what I understood about her right from the start. She was used to things. She *expected* things.

MARVIN. That's what good upbringing does for you.

BERNARD. It made her regal in my poor inner-city eyes.

MARVIN. You wanted Pam, Bernard. Habiba knew that. That's why she didn't put up a fight for you.

BERNARD. But, I married an illusion, a dream.

MARVIN. Habiba was the illusion, brother.

BERNARD. I lied to Habiba. I lied to Pam. I've lied to myself. Whatever happens, happens, I don't care anymore.

MARVIN. You know what's bugging you? You're ashamed to admit that you preferred Pam because she was pretty, rich, and had light skin. You feel guilty because you rejected dark Habiba. That's it, isn't it? *Isn't it?*

> *Bernard says nothing.*

You think you're the first? Shit, I can promise you you won't be the last. Oh, man, it wasn't just her skin color. It was everything about her. Her taste. Her *class*, brother. That's what attracted you. In the long run, you knew you could take Pam anywhere. She has the flexibility to be anything and look any kind of way. That's why you wanted her. She can fit in. Need her to be the perfect hostess for the sales reps coming to see you at your home, she can do that; want to go see a Broadway musical that hasn't a thing to do with the race problem, Pam'll be right there. Need that perfect wife to razzle dazzle the corporate execs at the next Broadcasters Convention, hey,

Pam'll be johnny on the spot. Habiba didn't have that flexibility. You knew it even back then. That's why you left her, man. You were becoming too sophisticated to get locked into doing things one way, and one way only.

BERNARD. She died, man. Killed fighting a revolution; fighting for a cause. That was no illusion. That was real.

MARVIN. Her reality, not yours. You have to be practical, Bernard. Even if your big house and social status seem insignificant right now, you just remember that you didn't even have that much back in those good old days you want to run back to. Whether you admit it or not, all that talk we did about freedom, justice, and equality— all that marching and singing; all those sacrifices, the injuries—all those *deaths*—pointed to just one thing: not black nationhood, but a nice home in a nice neighborhood, two cars, a fine family, money in the bank, and a chance at the good life.

And if you think I'm lying, just take a look at how all your great revolutionary leaders in Africa live once they get to power. Show me one successful black American leader who still lives in the ghetto. Show me one welfare mother who wouldn't leap at the chance to escape the inner city Habiba loved so much if she could just get her hands on half the money you make in just one year. Pam under-stands that, and that's why you went after her. 'Cause she's got the class and she's got the knowledge. And face it, brotha, that's what you wanted all along, isn't it? That's what any sensible man wants. Isn't it, brotha? Isn't it? …Well, isn't it?

BERNARD. No. A purpose, Marvin. Something worth living for, fighting for, and, if need be, worth dying for. That's what any sensible man wants. Especially any sensible black man.

> *Bernard gulps down his drink, slams the glass down on the bar, and exits, leaving Marvin to ponder.*

Scene 18

Lights up on Tanya's apartment. Pam appears at the door and rings the doorbell. Tanya answers it and comes face to face with Pam.

PAM. Tanya Blakely?

TANYA. Look, I don't want any trouble…

PAM. Then you know who I am.

TANYA. Yes.

PAM. May I come in?

TANYA. I told you, I don't want any trouble.

PAM. It's a little late to be worrying about causing any trouble, isn't it? May I come in?

Tanya steps back and Pam enters.

May I sit down?

TANYA. Oh, you plan to be here that long?

PAM. May I sit down?

Pam sits. Tanya sits across from her.

TANYA. Well?

PAM. Looking at you, I see why my husband is so taken with you. I may as well admit it. He's probably in love with you.

TANYA. Yes, he probably is.

PAM. Are you in love with him?

TANYA. Yes. I am.

PAM. Then we have a problem.

TANYA. We don't have a problem. He's not in love with you, anymore.

PAM. He's told you that?

TANYA. He will.

PAM. You have a lot to learn about Bernard, my dear.

TANYA. How did you find me?

PAM. Sometimes it's necessary to invade your husband's privacy to learn more about him.

Tanya says nothing.

I'm here to tell you that I'm not giving him up.

TANYA. I consider myself warned. Now, if you'll excuse me—

PAM. You and I are not through, yet.

TANYA. Oh yes we are—

PAM. Sit down.

TANYA. What makes you think you can boss me around in my own house?

PAM. There are rules, Miss Blakely. You know them as well as I do. I'm not the one trying to steal somebody's husband.

Tanya sits.

TANYA. I don't have to steal him. He'll come willingly.

PAM. And how long will he stay? Do you really think he'll give you the same number of years he gave me?

TANYA. The same, and more.

PAM. What are you? Twenty-four? Twenty-five?

TANYA. Old enough.

PAM. I'm forty-one. I've stood with him at the funerals of both his parents and had him at my side when each of our four children were born. I gave him the money to publish his first book of poetry and flew to Africa with him and stood at the grave of the only woman I think he ever truly loved. I've watched him suffer the indignities of being subordinate to people who didn't have one-tenth his talent or intellect. I've forgotten more about him than you'll ever learn.

TANYA. So?

PAM. I'm here to tell you you're in way over your head.

TANYA. Am I? All I ever had to do was be patient and the man was mine. He's been primed to leave you for years. He was just waiting for the right woman to come along.

PAM. And you think you're that woman?

TANYA. I *know* I am. And I'll have babies for him, too. And hold his hands and do everything for him you did, and more.

PAM. I'll bet you would if you had the chance.

TANYA. I will have the chance. Or else you wouldn't be here.

PAM. *(Rises.)* How far will you go for him, Tanya? Tell me that? How much of yourself will you give up? How much pain can you stand? I look at you and I wonder…

TANYA. You don't have to wonder about me. Anything you can do, I can do. Anything you know, I know, too. Alright?

PAM. See, that's not even what I'm talking about. I see a strong will, but I don't see character. Do you know what pressure is, honey?

TANYA. Go home.

PAM. Disappointment, perhaps? I mean, real disappointment— not just a canceled gold card or some other buppie shit. But real disappointment. What do you really know about Bernard besides that sliver of meat that hangs between his legs?

TANYA. Get out.

PAM. Do you know about the torment that burns inside their souls? Can you go into that white heat and cool it down? You'll have to do that a lot with Bernard, you know.

TANYA. Get out, I said.

PAM. I was frightened, coming here. I want you to know that. Terribly frightened.

TANYA. I don't give a damn. You need to be frightened.

PAM. Then, I saw you and it all came together. I know, now, I don't have to be afraid any longer. You'll send him back to me.

TANYA. All my life I've had to deal with stuck-up yella bitches like you. Y'all think you're God's gift, with your sense of tradition and your money, and your mixed heritage and all that other shit. I've watched you all get by on nothing more than your looks. What blondes are to brunettes you bitches are to us. Well, I got your man, honey. Little old black-as-night me and I'm gonna keep him. I don't care how much you know about him, or how many kids y'all got. I don't care if you win every penny in the divorce settlement. I'll still have *him*. And whatever he loses I'll build back up for him *double*.

And that means twice as much money, twice as many kids, and twice as much *woman*.

> *Pam says nothing. She rises and goes to the door. She stops and turns.*

PAM. It's not a new woman he's looking for, Tanya. Ask him about Habiba.

> *Pam turns and goes out. Tanya stands watching, puzzled by the comment. She picks up a pillow and throws it with all her might in the direction Pam has exited.*
>
> *Lights.*

Scene 19

> *Lights up on Pam and Bernard. At home.*

BERNARD. So I'm signing over the bulk of our stock portfolio to you; all of our jointly held accounts and the money market accounts. If it's alright with you, I want to keep the savings account and the mutual bonds for myself.

PAM. Will we need lawyers?

BERNARD. That's up to you.

PAM. And how do we explain this to the children?

BERNARD. I don't know. Tell them the truth, I guess.

PAM. And just what is the truth, Bernard?

BERNARD. I don't love you anymore.

PAM. Did you ever love me?

BERNARD. Yes.

PAM. Why did you stop?

BERNARD. I was lost. I had to find my way.

PAM. And Tanya's the way?

BERNARD. You had no right to go see her, Pam.

PAM. Don't tell me about what's right, Bernard.

BERNARD. I'm the one causing you pain, not her.

PAM. Don't you stand there and defend that bitch to me. Don't you dare!

BERNARD. We never should have been married. We're too different.

PAM. We're exactly what the other wanted.

BERNARD. I was wrong.

PAM. I was right.

BERNARD. Pamela—

PAM. Maybe I should let you go. Maybe I'm just holding on out of false pride, or ego, or maybe I'm just in some weird state of shock.

BERNARD. I'm sorry.

PAM. I just don't understand how you could have done it.

BERNARD. Look, let's just stop it here. I don't want to go any further into this.

PAM. Well, I do.

BERNARD. Pam—

PAM. No! Seventeen years of my life went into this marriage. And every day of those seventeen years I proceeded on the assumption that I had your love and that I could trust you. My faith was tied up in our loving each other; in the idea that ours was a commitment to each other, to our children, to our very future. Everything you've done, everything you've said to me over these years is called into question now because you've lied, Bernard. It's all been lies. You're sorry? That's not good enough.

BERNARD. What else can I say?

PAM. I don't know.

BERNARD. Look, I didn't deliberately plot to marry you, deceive you for seventeen years, and then suddenly run off at the age of forty-one with another woman. I didn't sit down one day and plot that scenario out.

PAM. No. You didn't plot anything. You've just allowed things to happen. I can see that.

BERNARD. So, you hate me.

PAM. I pity you.

BERNARD. Look, Pam, this isn't getting us anywhere. I don't want to argue.

PAM. I do.

BERNARD. Pam—

PAM. No, I want to know the truth. For once in your life, look me in the face and tell me everything. No lies, no metaphors, no little jokes, no pleasantries, no Mr. Nice Guy Bernard—just the *truth*!

BERNARD. Alright. I'm a coward. You're right. I couldn't tell you about my feelings because I didn't see how I had the right. A man is responsible to his family. A man is supposed to protect his own; provide for them. His family is his life. His family is the chain that binds him to his past and to his future. That's what I was taught. That's the way I was raised. You don't just walk up to your wife one day without provocation and announce that you're seeing someone else and you've fallen in love with that person, and you're going to leave to be with that other person. On what grounds?

You were never hateful, you were not unfaithful. There is not a single concrete reason I had in my mind for leaving you, no matter how I felt about Tanya. I have a seventeen-year investment in love, sacrifice, and blood here in this family. You don't turn your back on that. So, even after our oldest was born and I knew that I didn't love you as much as I should have, I figured that, in time, I would love you as much as I needed to. So, I waited and I tried and three more kids came. And my career started to take off—and suddenly I had money, status, position, a beautiful wife, four lovely kids, a great house, two cars, the picket fence, the whole works! And there was nothing left of me! Pamela, I didn't get fired from the station. I resigned. I no longer had my own life. I was living your life and the kids' lives, and the life that our families expected me to live. I had to find a way out. I couldn't take it any-more. I didn't have the guts to come right out and say it so I created a set of circumstances in which the destruction of all this was inevitable. That's why I never really tried to find another job; that's why I never lifted a finger to do anything that would get that yoke back around my neck. I destroyed everything and out of those ashes, maybe I can start over again. I'm going to rebuild my life, the way I intended to in the beginning. And maybe this time I won't be such a coward. Maybe this time I'll be able to look the world right in the eye for a change.

PAM. *(After a beat.)* How I hate you. When I think of all that I was prepared to go through to keep you...

BERNARD. Don't try to make me out to be the villain in all this, Pam. You did a lot of playacting yourself. You're not entirely blameless in this.

PAM. No, I'm not. In my case, it's an error of judgment. And that poor little Tanya, she just let her behind overrule her mind, but you—you knew every step of the way, exactly what was happening and exactly what you were doing. I guess that's why, when I saw her, I realized that you didn't love Tanya, either. No matter what you say, Bernard. You don't love her.

BERNARD. How do you know what I feel?

PAM. Didn't you just hear what I said? I saw her. Think about it. How do you think she'll feel when she finds out?

BERNARD. *(Tense.)* Finds out what?

PAM. She's the spitting image of Habiba.

> *Bernard says nothing.*

She'll hate you for trying to turn her into something she's not. And you can't make up for Habiba no matter how hard you try.

BERNARD. I'm not trying to make up for anything.

PAM. Will you have children?

BERNARD. I don't know if I want children.

PAM. I'll bet she does. That fool girl has no idea what she's getting herself into.

BERNARD. I don't need to hear this.

PAM. Men never do. Men love their illusions. It's women who have to deal with the truth, because we have to live with the consequences of male folly. We're the ones who have to clean up the messes you make. We wipe your asses when you're babies and cover your asses when you're grown.

BERNARD. That's enough!

PAM. Yes. Finally, it is, isn't it?

BERNARD. I'm going upstairs…talk to the kids…

PAM. They love you very much. Don't cut yourself out of their lives.

BERNARD. I won't.

PAM. You can come see them whenever you want. I won't stand in your way.

BERNARD. Goodbye, Pam.

PAM. Bernard?…

>*He turns.*

Be happy… Be happy…

>*Lights.*

Scene 20

>*Two months later. Tanya's apartment. Bernard is hard at work, going over papers scattered around him. He consults a few notes, then makes an entry on a laptop computer.*

>*Tanya enters from outside, carrying a briefcase and elegantly dressed in a business suit. Bernard gives no notice of her presence. She watches him in silence before continuing into the room.*

TANYA. Hi.

BERNARD. *(Looking up.)* Oh. Hey, baby. Didn't hear you come in.

TANYA. Tired.

BERNARD. Long day, huh?

TANYA. Something like that.

>*Bernard grunts a reply and goes deeper into his work. Tanya kicks off her shoes, tosses off her coat, and lays her briefcase aside.*

I hope that's a résumé you're typing.

BERNARD. You just got home and you want to start, already?

TANYA. I'm really tired of this: You haven't worked in two months, Bernard.

BERNARD. I've got money saved. I need time to work my plans out.

TANYA. Rent and expenses are going up.

BERNARD. I've *got* money.

Bernard continues writing. Tanya stares at him.

TANYA. I know your divorce is putting a lot of pressure on you—the separation from your kids and all—but you and I are supposed to be building a life together and—

BERNARD. Here. Read this.

He motions her over to the computer and she studies the screen.

It's a proposal. I'm flying down to New Orleans to present it at the African-American Commerce Convention.

TANYA. The Diaspora Group?

BERNARD. That's what I'm going to call the consortium that I'll put together to challenge for control of Griggs Broadcasting.

TANYA. Oh… *(Moving away.)* I would have thought you'd given up on that by now.

BERNARD. It's worth fighting for, Tanya.

TANYA. So is our relationship.

BERNARD. What's that supposed to mean?

TANYA. You're spending money you don't have to go down to New Orleans to present a proposal for a business arrangement that's hopeless, at best.

BERNARD. It's not hopeless. Griggs hasn't signed, yet.

TANYA. It's just a matter of time.

BERNARD. Then I'll make the most of whatever time I have.

TANYA. Fine. Do whatever you want.

She sits away from him, staring off. Bernard goes back to his work, then looks up. He watches her in silence for a moment, rises, and goes to a closet. He removes a package from the closet.

BERNARD. I bought this for you.

He brings the package to her.

TANYA. What is it?

BERNARD. Open it.

She opens the package. It is several yards of kente cloth. An African fabric. Tanya tenses.

TANYA. *(Half-hearted.)* It's beautiful, Bernard…so expensive…

BERNARD. Don't worry about it, baby. Just enjoy it. Hold still.

He starts to wrap it around her waist. She tries to back away.

Wait…

He finishes. Tanya is quite agitated, but says nothing.

There. You look beautiful.

TANYA. Your wife told me you had a friend who died in Africa. You went to her funeral.

BERNARD. Yes, that's true.

TANYA. Can I take it off, now?

BERNARD. No. Wear it awhile.

TANYA. *(Emphatic.)* I want it off. Now!

Tanya undoes the dress and moves away from him.

BERNARD. Now, what's wrong?

Tanya picks up the kente cloth and holds it out to him.

TANYA. You think I don't know what this represents…and who?

BERNARD. It's just a dress.

TANYA. A funeral in Africa…the Diaspora Group…kente cloth… I will not be the surrogate for a dead woman, Bernard!

BERNARD. Is that what you think?

TANYA. What else am I supposed to think?!

BERNARD. I admit I wish you could be like her, but I have never wanted you to be her.

TANYA. I have given you everything. I have torn out my guts for you. I have withstood all of your hang-ups, your temper tantrums, the changes you went through with your wife—and now you do me like this!

BERNARD. Tanya, calm down…

TANYA. No!

BERNARD. Calm down, I said.

TANYA. I have memories, too, Bernard! But your halcyon days were not mine! I carry the memories of a seven-year-old girl in Newark standing in food lines because rioters burned down the only supermarket our people had. I had to crawl around the floor on my stomach because the state troopers were shooting through the windows of our apartment, thinking we were snipers. A cousin of mine was killed on the street. *Friends* of mine were killed. And all during that time, I didn't see one dashiki. Not one headwrap. Not one militant brother and sister in the streets, prepared to lead us, or risk anything for us. After all their spouting ideology, all their rantings and ravings about "whitey" and smashing the "power structure," when crunch time came, it was the brothers in the do-rags and the sisters in the miniskirts and clog shoes who did the dying while all the revolutionaries were safely hidden away.

And so that seven-year-old girl made up her mind, and went to school and got her degree. And she presses her hair and goes to work every day and keeps her mouth shut…because *that's* how you get ahead…and *that's* how you stay alive in this white man's country. *(Looks at the kente cloth again.)* Why is she so important? She's dead! She can't love you. She can't hold you. She can't comfort you. There's nothing she can do for you. A dead woman with dead ideas! She failed you, Bernard. All those days were a failure. Nothing was accomplished. *Nothing!*

BERNARD. Everything I ever started out to be in my life is tied up in Habiba's memory, Tanya. I won't give her up.

TANYA. You talk as though you think you owe her something. What? What do you owe her? Everything you've done with your life, you've done on your own. The same with me. This is OUR life, Bernard. We're free to live it the way we want to. We've worked hard—

BERNARD. We all have to give back. Sooner or later. No matter how far, or how fast we climb. It's always been that way. We're the lucky ones. Dr. Du Bois called us the Talented Tenth; the ones who were expected to build the ladder for our people to climb. The old folks used to talk about Race Men and Race Women. It didn't matter where you went to school, or how rich you became. You could even become president of the United States, or sit on the Supreme Court.

The bottom line was always the same: helping the Race. Making our people's lives better. When my children look into my face I wonder what they see. I was supposed to have passed on a legacy to them. I'm not sure I did my job, Tanya. Malcolm and Dr. King died for something more than BMWs and la bon vie… And if you can't understand that…

TANYA. Oh, like Pam understood? Let you use me up for the next seventeen years till one day you run into some young broad who looks like your friendly ghost and you decide to leave me for her?

BERNARD. You haven't heard a word I've said.

TANYA. I will not have my life sucked up by a ghost. Either you see me for who I am or leave me the hell alone!

BERNARD. I know the difference between fantasy and reality, Tanya. I see you…maybe too well…

TANYA. And I see you, too: a middle-aged man, filling his head up with a whole lot of stupid dreams and ideas, trying to relive his youth!

BERNARD. If those words were meant to hurt me, you've succeeded.

TANYA. I don't know what I ever saw in you.

BERNARD. Then we're both the poorer for it, Tanya.

TANYA. Damn you! Goddamn you!

She pulls the engagement ring from her finger and hurls it at him, then turns and flees the room.

Lights shift. Segue.

Scene 21

A few weeks later, Griggs and Bernard at Eagle Rock.

BERNARD. Thanks for agreeing to see me.

GRIGGS. Talk to me. This is a nice view, but I've seen it before.

BERNARD. I hear you haven't closed with Pegasus.

GRIGGS. Just a matter of time.

BERNARD. Don't. Make the deal with me, instead.

GRIGGS. We've been through this.

BERNARD. Then, we'll go through it again.

GRIGGS. That won't be necessary.

BERNARD. It'll be as necessary as I want it to be, goddammit. If anybody's gonna run Griggs Broadcasting after you, it's gonna be me.

GRIGGS. I hear emotion, I hear rhetoric. I don't hear reality. You're wasting my time, Bernard.

Griggs starts off.

BERNARD. I've got the Diaspora Group behind me, Sam. We're prepared to match the offer from Pegasus…and we'll go higher, if we have to.

Griggs stops, turns.

GRIGGS. Why should I give up a bird in the hand for some idealistic Negroes in the bush?

BERNARD. Pegasus will erase every memory of you once they get their hands on your company, and you know it. And you didn't build that business for that to happen.

GRIGGS. And neither did I build my business to be run by an insufferable, idealistic, sentimental, hot-tempered pain in the ass.

BERNARD. Yes, but I'm *your* idealistic, sentimental, hot-tempered pain in the ass, and that's why you'll make this deal with me. Because you know I'll remember every lesson you ever taught me and I'll do anything to keep our legacy alive…and when the time comes, I'll pass it on to the *next* idealistic, sentimental, hot-tempered pain in the ass. Now, you tell me: Will Pegasus make you the same promise?

GRIGGS. God, how I want to believe you, Bernard…but you made a mess of your life—both professional and personal.

BERNARD. It's a price I had to pay. Somewhere along the line I forgot I was generation number six. But now I want to think all the pain and tears were worth it, if for no other reason than I finally found out what it was I always wanted: that sense of commitment to something beyond myself. It feels good to do that again…

There was a woman I loved very deeply. The same year she died, the Movement died. All the values we believed in, all the youthful fire, all the innocence—just seemed to disappear. We all became willing to settle for just a little bit less; willing to compromise just to be able to have some peace and quiet.

And for twenty years we've been lost. I've been lost. Not anymore. Through her, I've made my peace. With my past, with my present. I know who I am, I know what I want and I know where I'm going...

GRIGGS. Maybe it's a trip we can make together.

Griggs comes to Bernard and extends his hand. They shake. They have a deal.

Lights.

Scene 22

Lights up on Bernard's office at Griggs Broadcasting. Bernard goes over some papers as a young black man, about twenty-two years old, enters.

BERNARD. Graduated top of your class in Howard's "B" school. Outstanding.

YOUNG MAN. You didn't come to the graduation party. I missed you.

BERNARD. Your mom and me... Well, it might have been awkward... You get my present?

YOUNG MAN. Yes.

Beat.

That doctor's pressing her to marry him.

BERNARD. No one pressures your mother into anything. Whatever decision she makes will be the right one.

YOUNG MAN. You should tell her that, Dad. I think she'd like to hear it from you.

BERNARD. Your mother and I talk... It's always good to hear her voice.

YOUNG MAN. You're like a legend in Howard's "B" school. I was proud.

BERNARD. I'm too young to be a legend. I'm putting you in the sales department, selling air time.

YOUNG MAN. Coolie work?! I'm your son. How'm I gonna make any money?

BERNARD. That's your goal in life?

YOUNG MAN. It better be.

BERNARD. It's a desire, not a goal.

YOUNG MAN. Sometimes, for black people, our desires and our goals have to be one and the same.

Bernard looks at him.

Don't look at me like that. It's a new age, Dad. These days, people may be race conscious, but they're just not as race-oriented as they were in your day. Big difference. You know?

BERNARD. And how would you know, Peachfuzz? You just got here.

YOUNG MAN. I know I can relax a lot more in my life than you and Mom could in yours.

BERNARD. Now, you listen to me: You're the seventh generation since slavery. You're the smartest, fastest, most educated generation we've produced yet. But you're not free...and you can't relax. Your trouble will always come when you begin to think that you deserve a good time, when you begin to think that this world is your oyster. Your children can have the good time, not you. For you, there's only struggle. Understand?

Lights change. Bernard steps back into the darkness. A spot begins shining on the young man.

YOUNG MAN. You scared me when you said that.

BERNARD. *(Receding into the darkness.)* I know.

YOUNG MAN. I've been scared ever since.

BERNARD. Well, don't be scared, youngblood. Just be ready.

Bernard disappears into the darkness, leaving the young man in the spot. Then the spot fades to blackness.

End of Play

PROPERTY LIST
(Use this space to create props lists for your production)

SOUND EFFECTS
(Use this space to create sound effects lists for your production)

Note on Songs/Recordings, Images, or Other Production Design Elements

Be advised that Dramatists Play Service, Inc., neither holds the rights to nor grants permission to use any songs, recordings, images, or other design elements mentioned in the play. It is the responsibility of the producing theater/organization to obtain permission of the copyright owner(s) for any such use. Additional royalty fees may apply for the right to use copyrighted materials.

For any songs/recordings, images, or other design elements mentioned in the play, works in the public domain may be substituted. It is the producing theater/organization's responsibility to ensure the substituted work is indeed in the public domain. Dramatists Play Service, Inc., cannot advise as to whether or not a song/arrangement/recording, image, or other design element is in the public domain.

9780822238973